IAIN SINCLAIR

IAIN
SINCLAIR

Robert Sheppard

NORTHCOTE

BRITISH
COUNCIL

© Copyright 2007 by Robert Sheppard
First published in 2007 by Northcote House Publishers Ltd, Horndon, Tavistock,
Devon, PL19 9NQ, United Kingdom.
Tel: +44 (0) 1822 810066 Fax: +44 (0) 1822 810034.

British Library Cataloguing-in-Publication Data
A catalogue record for this book is available from the British Library

ISBN 978-0-7463-1149-3 hardcover
      978-0-7463-1154-7 paperback
Typeset by PDQ Typesetting, Newcastle-under-Lyme
Printed and bound in the United Kingdom

Contents

Acknowledgements   vii

Biographical Outline   viii

Abbreviations and References   x

Introduction. Logging the Contour Lines of Culture   1

1   Poetry: The Hard Stuff. The Toffee of the Universe   25

2   Mere Fiction (i.e. it hasn't happened yet)   42

    White Chappell, Scarlet Tracings
    Downriver
    Landor's Tower

3   Ambulatory Documentary: From Stalker to Fugueur 83

Notes   94

Select Bibliography   100

Index   111

Acknowledgements

The author and publisher would like to thank Iain Sinclair for permission to quote from his published works, and for answering the author's small number of questions of a factual nature. The author is grateful to the Edge Hill University Research Development Fund for financial assistance in the completion of this work. I would like to thank Patricia Farrell and Stephen H. Gregg for discussing this work with me.

Biographical Outline

1943	Iain MacGregor Sinclair born in Cardiff on 11 June. Father is a doctor, mother a former doctors' pharmacist. Grows up in Maesteg, South Wales.
1956–61	Educated at Cheltenham College.
1962	Attends London School of Film Technique, Electric Avenue, Brixton.
1962–6	Attends Trinity College Dublin; English and Fine Arts BA.
1967	Makes Allen Ginsberg television documentary *Ah! Sunflower!* for West German TV. Marries Mary Annabel Rose (Anna) Hadman; three children: Farne (1972), William Llewelyn (1975) and Madeleine (1980).
1967–70	Residence on Gozo (Malta).
1968	Corresponds with William Burroughs over a scripted but unshot documentary film, *The Face on the Fork*.
1968–70	Works at North East London College and School of Art in Waltham Forest lecturing in General Studies and, later, Film. Teaches the sculptor Brian Catling there.
1969	Moves to Hackney. Various short-term local jobs, including cigar packer and brewery worker.
1970–79	Establishes Albion Village Press. Publishes important works by Chris Torrance, Brian Catling, J. H. Prynne, Peter Riley, Renchi Bicknell, and Sinclair himself.
1972	Attends the Courtauld Institute, London, for a term, to study towards an MA in Fine Arts.
1974	Works as garden assistant for Tower Hamlets Council.
1975–	Career as book dealer, now occasional; 1975–87:

	street market (Camden Passage, Islington); 1987–95: book fairs and mail order catalogues.
1987	*White Chappell, Scarlet Tracings* is sole runner-up for the Guardian Fiction Prize.
1990–93	Poetry editor at Paladin Books. Oversees the publication of several volumes, including *The Tempers of Hazard* (Thomas A. Clark, Barry MacSweeney, Chris Torrance) and *Future Exiles* (Allen Fisher, Bill Griffiths, Brian Catling).
1991	Curates the *Shamanism of Intent* exhibition at the Goldmark Gallery, Uppingham.
1992	*Downriver* wins the James Tait Black Memorial Prize and the Encore Award (for the year's Best Second Novel); runner-up for the Guardian Fiction Prize.
1990s	Works as a self-employed writer, while also making documentary films, reviewing and broadcasting.
2002	Delivers the George Orwell Lecture, Birkbeck College.
2002	Organizes the Barbican event *London Orbital* to launch the book and film of that name.
2003	Begins to reside for part of the year in St Leonards, East Sussex.

Abbreviations and References

C	*Crash* (London: BFI Publications, 1999)
DR	*Downriver* (London: Paladin, 1991)
DS	*Dining on Stones* (London: Hamish Hamilton, 2004)
FESM	*Flesh Eggs & Scalp Metal: Selected Poems 1970–87* (London: Paladin, 1989)
KMD	*The Kodak Mantra Diaries* (London: Albion Village Press, 1971)
LC	*Liquid City* (London: Reaktion Books, 1999)
LHSB	*Lud Heat/Suicide Bridge* (London: Vintage, 1995)
LO	*London Orbital* (London: Granta, September 2002)
LOT	*Lights Out for the Territory* (London: Granta, 1997)
LT	*Landor's Tower* (London: Granta, 2001)
RD	*Radon Daughters* (London: Jonathan Cape, 1994)
RR	*Rodinsky's Room* (London: Granta, 1999)
SCA	*Slow Chocolate Autopsy* (London: Weidenfeld, 1997)
SM	*Sorry Meniscus* (London: Profile Books, 1999)
SS	Arthur Conan Doyle, *A Study in Scarlet* (London: Penguin, 2001)
V	*The Verbals* (Tonbridge: Worple Press, 2003)
WCST	*White Chappell, Scarlet Tracings* (London and Glasgow: Paladin, 1988)
WG	*White Goods* (Uppingham: Goldmark, 2002)

Introduction: Logging the Contour Lines of Culture

If all of Iain Sinclair's books are 'book-length footnotes to his other books', as Nicholas Lezard contends, then it is necessary to outline the extent of the resultant entangled web.[1] Intertextuality is a term first defined by Julia Kristeva to account for the perception that 'any text is constructed as a mosaic of quotations; any text is the absorption and transformation of another', and has been more generally used to describe the ways in which an author's text will beg, borrow and steal from the texts of others, indeed may be largely constituted by these webs of connection.[2] While a range of intertextual strategies abound in Sinclair's work, the word 'intratext' might more accurately describe the way his poetry, fiction and non-fiction of the last thirty years is cross-referential, and how any part of this *oeuvre* may be connected to any other, as Lezard teasingly suggests. It is, to use the vocabulary of Deleuze and Guattari, a rhizome, a non-hierarchical interconnected, growing, but sometimes contradictory, whole.[3] To recognize the work in this way is important since my study will otherwise read his work by genre. The sense of connectivity – in terms of collage and juxtaposition – is not just the *modus operandi* of this work; it also informs how Sinclair has constructed a rule of thumb cultural theory, one to which I shall return several times.

Appropriately it was as an intertextual footnote that Sinclair first made his mark in the official world of letters. Turning to the back of Peter Ackroyd's *Hawksmoor* (1985), inquisitive readers would have found a note informing them that the book's central conceit, the identification of occult powers emanating from the configuration of Hawkmoor's London churches, was derived

1

from the odd-sounding book of poems and prose, *Lud Heat*, which Iain Sinclair had published in 1975. Ackroyd knew of this work because, like Sinclair, he had until this time been a member of a poetic avant-garde within which Sinclair's poetry was well regarded. In fact as early as 1976 one important little magazine, *Poetry Information*, had no difficulty in dubbing Sinclair 'one of the most distinctive new voices on the UK poetry, prose and publishing scene'.[4] Ackroyd's and Sinclair's involvements in what is now sometimes called the British Poetry Revival are quite different: in Ackroyd's case, he was in cultural and conservative alignment with French theory and the Cambridge poets, while Sinclair showed allegiance to the 1960s counter-culture and its post-Beat poetry. As the praise above suggests, Sinclair was also active as a small press publisher. Both *Lud Heat* and its follow-up, the even more menacingly entitled *Suicide Bridge* (1979), named after the bridge where the Kray gang dumped evidence after the murder of Jack 'the Hat' McVitie, were published by his own Albion Village Press (using unofficial nomenclature for the area of Hackney where Sinclair lives).

The two books were the first two parts of a 'triad'. *Lud Heat* tracks Sinclair's life as a London local council grass-cutter in delicate poems that often utilize what might be thought of as his earliest style: a verse open in form but closed in private reference, full of minatory dream imagery and mysticism, but held in tension with notations of domestic detail. These personal patterns are also traced upon larger psychic and geographical forces, once more negotiated in prose, particularly in the essay entitled 'Nicholas Hawksmoor, His Churches', which Ackroyd had found such a stimulus. This is accompanied by a map which traces lines – rather like ley lines – between such sites as St Anne's Limehouse and Christ Church Spitalfields, but also between literary sites such as the dwellings of Blake and Keats. *Suicide Bridge* presents a series of narratives in free verse about the 'Sons of Albion', borrowed from Blake's *Jerusalem*, but reborn as malevolent spirits of modern England (including the Kray twins), with meditations in prose on the relationship of myth to place.

A third part of the triad was announced, indeed its subject matter (an oblique investigation of the Jack the Ripper murders) was rehearsed in an interview as early as 1976, but it did not appear. In the late 1970s uncollected fragments of a *Suicide Bridge* book 2 were published in little magazines. In the early 1980s Sinclair published a number of chapbooks in editions of less than twenty, including *Autistic Poses* (1985), which features angry poems about the deprivation of the East End of London – one is even called 'Street Detail' – caused by the Conservative Thatcher government, which had come to power in 1979. Rejecting the mystical and the dream, and implicating himself in his analysis, Sinclair wrote of the 'dole-scratching, ill tempered lumpen/mess of what we are become' (*FESM* 145). The sense of disillusioned social and literary exclusion, in the title, the content, and in the expectations encoded in the limited print run of this booklet, offered no warning of what would happen next.

While there were narrative elements in *Suicide Bridge*, and prose essays amid the poems, the novel *White Chappell, Scarlet Tracings* seemed an unpredictable, as well as delayed, conclusion to the triad. Given its long gestation period, it is perhaps not surprising that it was largely written in six weeks. However, it brought Sinclair mainstream publication and launched his literary career as a novelist. First published by the private press Goldmark in 1987, it was republished later that year by Paladin. It was the sole runner-up for the Guardian Fiction Prize.

One of the direst rumours about Sinclair in the near-silence of the early 1980s was that he had given up writing (which was not true) and was working as a bookseller (which was true). It was this trade, and its grail-like pursuits of rare volumes that provided the contemporary characters for his first fiction. Sinclair has also spoken of this work as a 'second education' (*V* 105), during which he became aware of the 'lost books' of important prose writers of the past who had suffered a similar neglect to his contemporaries in the poetry world (*V* 103). Somewhat like Ackroyd's *Hawksmoor*, which won its author the Whitbread Prize, and established Ackroyd's position as the foremost novelist taking as his subject matter the variously connected histories and fictions of the city of London, *White Chappell, Scarlet Tracings* moves back and forth from the London of the past (in this case Victorian London) to a contemporary and a near-contemporary reality; it makes fictive play of the preposterous theories about the identity of Jack the Ripper. Yet the text wraps itself in a self-protective irony that places any of the 'mystical' or conspiratorial 'facts' under suspended suspicion. It is a tone that was to serve Sinclair well, an escape valve for his wilder speculations.

The rise of literary fiction in the 1980s, with its fabulist sense of history, was an apposite moment for the arrival of *White Chappell, Scarlet Tracings*. Ackroyd's *Hawksmoor* juxtaposes passages about the diabolic and anti-Enlightenment architect Dyer (really Hawksmoor) and a contemporary detective, also called Hawksmoor, whose rationalism slowly fails him as uncanny parallels between the two worlds collapse one reality into another. Salman Rushdie's *Midnight's Children*, which had won the Booker Prize in 1981, weaves a fantastic magic realist tale around the 'real' events of the granting of independence to India in 1947. Graham Swift's *Waterland* (1983) presents history, both personal and national, as a literary construct, reflecting the postmodernist sense that the grand narratives of history are no longer legitimate. It is not clear that Sinclair's novel was responding directly to these cultural trends, yet the insane book dealers of *White Chappell, Scarlet Tracings* at least regard such fiction as economic, if not cultural, capital: 'Oh Jesus, oh God! My *Waterland*'s been stolen' (WCST 40). Yet, unlike his earlier work, *White Chappell, Scarlet Tracings* now existed in a cultural environment which had begun to understand and value it. Ackroyd's appropriations may even have been the spur for Sinclair to write his own trans-historical novel. He has said: 'I never considered that my stuff had any commercial possibility until the 1980s when books like Peter Ackroyd's *Hawksmoor*, which made use of similar material to mine, were becoming very successful.'[5] Sinclair's attitude to Ackroyd is notably ambivalent, as a possible debt to him balances a possible grievance. There is nearly always a reference to Ackroyd in each of his books; in *White Chappell, Scarlet Tracings* the plot of Ackroyd's *Chatterton* (also published in 1987) is summarized by an avatar of Ackroyd, a deranged East End barman. 'Sinclair' and his accomplice, Joblard, escape from the pub, the author-narrator commenting, 'The terror. Now they are all writers; all rewriting the past' (WCST 66-7). In 'The Necromancer's A to Z', a review of Ackroyd's compendious history *London: The Biography* (2000), Sinclair, while full of praise for the detail of Ackroyd's book, is critical of his conservative rewriting of the distant past to anaesthetize the poll tax riots and race riots of the near-present, which Ackroyd presents as ephemeral distractions from the life story of the city.[6]

However, for contemporary models for Sinclair's entry into the world of fiction, one can best look to his earliest passion, the Beats, particularly to the extraordinary postmodern final trilogy of William Burroughs: *Cities of the Red Night*, *The Place of Dead Roads* and *The Western Lands*, published between 1981 and the year *White Chappell, Scarlet Tracings* appeared. Funny, fragmentary, multiple, conspiratorial, eclectic in mythological intertextual reference and self-referential in intratextual commentary, these novels arguably proved the most important inspiration, although they are rarely alluded to.

In 1991 Sinclair published *Downriver*, 'A Narrative in Twelve Tales' as the title page is keen to remind readers. The episodic nature of this long text – it eschews the title novel – seems appropriate to the richness of narrative content, and may have reminded contemporary taste of another novel to take history on an episodic fictive journey: Julian Barnes's *A History of the World in 10½ Chapters*, published two years before. The tales (none is discrete, but they overlap) range in tone from the conspiratorial to – a new element in Sinclair's work – the satirical: the account of the Widow's Monument is an apposite satire upon late Thatcherism, particularly as it impacted upon the Docklands Regeneration (which was a deregulated capitalist fiefdom). As in Ackroyd's 'biography', London is the book's protagonist, a psychological and geographical magnet which holds the various tales of terror, invasion, satirical excess and carnivalistic absurdity in one form. Written in a frantic five months of activity, it remains Sinclair's masterpiece in fiction.

Downriver won the James Tait Black Memorial Prize and the Encore Award as well as receiving excellent, but sometimes rather baffled, reviews; it received one each from London writers Michael Moorcock and Angela Carter, whose own capacious epic fantasies of London life had recently been published, respectively *Mother London* (1988) and *Wise Children* (1991). While there is no evidence of direct debt in *Downriver*, both writers are retrospectively acknowledged as kindred spirits by Sinclair in later book dedications.

In 1994, after a promising move to Jonathan Cape, Sinclair published *Radon Daughters*, announced as the third part of a second 'triad' which had begun with *White Chappell, Scarlet Tracings*. The disappearance of 'Sinclair' as a self-deprecating narrator, the unrelenting picaresque quest after an apocryphal horror text, the (unwritten) sequel to William Hope Hodgson's *House on the Borderland* (1908), and the attempt to feminize his hitherto rather male fictional world with rather implausible and unsympathetic female characters – the weather-girl/boxer Isabel/ Helen is particularly perplexing – make the book a less involving experience, a rather disappointing intratextual footnote to *Downriver*. The monopede bibliophile Todd Sileen is addicted to X-rays which give him visions, and he is recruited by a book collector, Drage-Bell, whose library is secreted near a Sweden-borgian outpost in London, to locate the Hodgson manuscript. As ever for Sinclair, possession of a divinatory text bestows power. Sileen's quest involves the triangulations of mounds at Whitechapel with those near the knowledge-centres of the universities of Oxford and Cambridge. Indeed, the Cambridge fellow Undark – an analogue for the poet J. H. Prynne – holds the occult text. Drage-Bell wants to read the text through Sileen's eyes and, under interrogation or irradiation, Sileen accesses some images from the non-existent manuscript. Sileen himself (who is a minor character in *Downriver*) is 'a character in Sammy Taylor's abandoned script, his actions dependent on that madman's whim' (*RD* 371). However, although Sileen is forging the art-hating Taylor's letters that lead the quest to an actual house on the borderland in Ireland, he is shot dead by the non-existent Taylor, an ironic revenge of the imagination. The key to the novel may indeed be Sileen's 'bibliography', reproduced near the book's end, for Sinclair's novel is a pastiche collaged from both high and low cultural sources in the consciousness (and listed in the bibliography) of Sileen himself. Among the many sources, there are near quotations from Flann O'Brien's *The Poor Mouth* (1941), as well as liftings from Tony Lambrianou's Kray gang memoir *Inside the Firm* (1991). Isabel muses on the book list: 'Why labour on when the bibliography is so much more interesting than the book?' (*RD* 44). The reading public agreed with this; *Radon Daughters* was not well received. 'It's strange,' Sinclair has reflected. 'It's the most fictional of all my books in its form ... but it's absolutely unreadable to the general reader' (*V* 128). There was to be no further novel until 2001.

Sinclair, who had slackened his book dealing, was increasingly making his living as a freelance writer by the 1990s. He began to receive commissions to write more regularly for newspapers like the *Guardian* and for journals like the *London Review of Books* as well as for specialist periodicals such as *Modern Painters*. The startling descriptive skills of the set pieces of his fiction – the piled epithets, the verbless sentences – were turned towards the contemporary world, but with a popular audience in mind. He began to appear regularly on television, sometimes in films made with Chris Petit, as a commentator on London and geographical matters, or on 'psychogeography' as the recycled Situationist term has it, the charting of connections between place and the people who traverse the territory.

In his essays, written out of walks across London, Sinclair and his companions reject the ambulatory gestures of the *flâneur*, wandering aimlessly, for that of the 'stalker': marching with determination along predetermined routes drawn on maps – like the Hawksmoor ley lines – to investigate certain pre-established hypotheses. The joys, though, are often the accidents, the messages that arise out of the experience, like sudden glimpses of 'oracular' graffiti. This could never be 'On the Road': the drunken swerve of the Beats or the cool Baudrillardian blur of traversing postmodern space. It maintains a focus upon the urban *pavement* and its subterranean layers: upon place, upon history, and their conjunction in the present.

The prose disarmingly conjures the same materials as the fiction, but in an explicatory way, thus extending and making complex the intratext of this work. Whereas certain artist-friends are mercilessly parodied in the fiction, they appear in their own guises in the documentary as important creative figures. He will juxtapose little-known London writers such as crime writer Derek Raymond and out-of-print Jewish novelist and poet Emanuel Litvinoff (he calls such cultural recovery 'the return of the reforgotten') with their notorious contemporaries, popular novelist and former Tory party chair Jeffrey Archer and drug dealer and raconteur Howard Marks.

These pieces were revised and collected by his new publisher, Granta, in *Lights Out for the Territory*, in 1997. *Lights Out* was an instant bestseller and its first edition was out of print within weeks. Once again, publication had proved timely, as critics had begun to speak of literary *non*-fiction, thus elevating such occasional writing to the status of a genre that was not simply journalism or belles-lettres. Writers such as Bruce Chatwin with *The Songlines* (1988) or Lorna Sage with *Bad Blood* (2000), in their different ways, were importing fictional devices into autobiography and the personal essay. However, thirty years earlier, the 'New Journalists', such as Hunter S. Thompson – who possibly had some impact on the growth of Sinclair's impressionistic style – used novelistic artifice in their journalism to create a mode of 'faction'. Indeed, it was Sinclair's prose style that was beginning to attract attention. James Wood began his review of *Lights Out* for the *Guardian*, with the accolade: 'Anyone who cares about English prose cares about Iain Sinclair ... He is a bitter, slangy, rich precisionist who is flooded with impressions.' [7]

But Sinclair was no stranger to documentary precision. In 1967 he had made a film, *Ah Sunflower!*, documented in his second published work, *The Kodak Mantra Diaries* (1971), which, along with Jeff Nuttall's *Bomb Culture* (1968), remains one of the best introductions to the British counter-culture. Central to the experience was the filming of prophetic ecologist Gregory Bateson, anti-psychiatrist R. D. Laing and Black Power leader Stokely Carmichael, amongst others, at the Dialectic of Liberation conference in London in 1967. Comparison with the Penguin Original collection of the conference proceedings, *Dialectic of Liberation* (1968), is instructive. [8] Sinclair not only shows the processes and compromises of filming the event, he exposes the contradictions and tensions of the counter-culture, mapped across his personal life. His long interview with Allen Ginsberg, of which he says, in *Lights Out*, 'Talking to him for a few days, gave me material to think about for years', was an experience where the objectivity of the documentarist broke down (*LOT* 280). For Ginsberg paraphrases the Black Mountain poet Charles Olson, 'Language is controlling [everybody] on a massive electronic scale', and comments, 'As this consciousness grows people start cutting out of the imagery that's being planted in their brains. Anybody is free to interpret history as he actually sees it so history becomes what happened, rather than what we are told is happening ... History is over,' Ginsberg concludes, with a more strategic sense of how to respond to the death of grand narratives than is found in later postmodernist thought. In his 2004 novel, *Dining on Stones*, Sinclair is still quoting, and thinking about, these lines. (*KMD* n.p., punctuation altered, quoted in *DS* 360) This gathering of 1960s radicals, with their liberatory and utopian rhetoric, sets the scene for Sinclair's restless grasping after alternative views and practices, whether they are the alternatives of the post-Beat poetry world of the 1960s, or the Burroughs-like paranoid sense of universal conspiracy (his next aborted film was to have been on Burroughs), or his later taste for off-beat gothic, or even the mysteries of a local character like David Rodinsky.

The late 1990s saw a flood of non-fiction books and collaborations by Sinclair, and one of the most fascinating, co-authored with the young artist Rachel Lichtenstein, was *Rodinsky's Room* (1999). Rodinsky had been a (real) character in *Downriver*, but with more of a walk-off than a walk-on part. Rodinsky, an Orthodox Jew living alone in a room above an abandoned synagogue in a three-storey Spitalfields house, seemed to have vanished, leaving behind a baffling array of Jewish hermetic texts, empty beer bottles, works of world linguistics, old newspapers, a Millet 'Angelus' calendar (for March 1963), and a suggestive *A-Z* of London marked with eccentric routes. The room was only opened in 1980. In *Downriver* elaborate fictions are woven around his absence. In *Rodinsky's Room* Sinclair introduces other Jewish analogues, the Hackney-born Harold Pinter or drug-taking actor David Litvin-off, but they are rather unconvincing. The book, even in terms of number of pages, belongs to Lichtenstein. While Sinclair is dedicated to keeping Rodinsky dematerialized as a malleable myth, it is Lichtenstein who re-materializes Rodinsky as a Jewish mystic, through a personal discovery of her Jewishness that takes her to Israel, and, harrowingly, to the Holocaust sites of Eastern Europe, before it reaches the materiality of Rodinsky's grave in the edge-lands of London. Such rematerialization also reveals a life of tragic deprivation and mental illness. However, the allure of the story is such that, armed with Rodinsky's *A–Z*, Sinclair walked the notations in the book, and published yet another book-length footnote to the man's barely visible life, *Dark Lanthorns: David Rodinsky as Psychogeographer* (1999). Peter

Barry, in recognizing that this book returns to the focus of *Lud Heat*, points out that 'Rodinsky is cast as an anticipatory avatar' of Sinclair himself, in that 'this is what Sinclair does, inscribing his own mental biro-lines on the tarmac, and then excavating and linking up the marked spots'.[9] Marc Atkins, who joined Sinclair on the walks of *Lights Out* and some in *Dark Lanthorns*, is rewarded with *Liquid City* (1999), which consists mainly of his photographs with short accompanying notational texts by Sinclair. He depicts the grim semi-industrial abandon of some of their walks, with portraits of many of the characters of the non-fiction (and fiction): from novelist Kathy Acker and guitarist-bookseller Martin Stone, through Ackroyd and Moorcock encountering one another in the blurry ambience of an alcoholically fuelled restaurant meal, to images of spectral poets at the launch of Sinclair's poetry anthology *Conductors of Chaos*.

Sinclair was poetry editor at Paladin in the early 1990s, a position he used generously to attempt to gain visibility for poets with whom he had been associated in the British Poetry Revival: the poet of place Allen Fisher – *Place* was even the title of a project that occupied him throughout the 1970s – or Sinclair's friend the sculptor (and by the 1990s, performance artist) Brian Catling, or the anarchist poet Bill Griffiths, all three of whom shared the Paladin volume of London poets, *Future Exiles* (1992). Along with other volumes in the series was a publication of Sinclair's own, *Flesh Eggs & Scalp Metal: Selected Poems 1970-1987* (1989), which made public early work and the near-samizdat publications of the 1980s. A further selection in *Penguin Modern Poets 10* (1996), a volume he shared with Douglas Oliver and Denise Riley, collected poems from the small press pamphlets *Jack Elam's Other Eye* (1991) and *The Ebbing of the Kraft* (1997); later poems are found in *Saddling the Rabbit* and *White Goods* (both 2002) and in *Buried at Sea* (2006). The occasional documentary low-life poems of the 1980s give way, in the 1990s, to oblique and opaque poems that often amount to lists of images and impressions. Ambivalence towards conventional syntax, worrying at the problematics of connectivity, reveal an intuitively collagist and modernist sensibility. Poems shy away from the definitiveness of the completed sentence, as though this were the province of (his) prose alone. In a public situation where the prose works are entering the mainstream, the poetry becomes private, in danger of extinction. 'I had always imagined there/would be no more poetry no readership,' one poem comments, but Sinclair immediately juxtaposes this meditation with an image with which it has no (logical) connection, in a late Black Mountain fashion: 'sailing proud, dust lilies in petrol water', a scene that is beneath 'a fishy/odourless sky' (*WG* 18). Such cherished images of blight, familiar from the non-fiction and from the photographs of Atkins, recur throughout these poems, as does the same cast of heroes and villains.

Sinclair's involvement with millionaire Mike Goldmark, *White Chappell, Scarlet Tracings'* first publisher, led to an attempt to relive one of the triumphs of the pre-*Kodak Mantra Diaries* literary underground, the Royal Albert Hall poetry reading of 1965. Thirty years later the rerun was not so auspicious, although 'the evening closed with Ginsberg duetting (the Chas 'n' Dave of the counter-culture) with Paul McCartney', as Sinclair sardonically records (*LOT* 159). Many of the performers (and some of the poets mentioned in the previous paragraph) were featured in Sinclair's anthology *Conductors of Chaos* (1996). The extraordinary young deaf performance poet Aaron Williamson – Sinclair narrates his introduction to the work by Catling in *Lights Out* – joins older British Poetry Revival poets such as J. H. Prynne or Lee Harwood (his early-sixties East End poem 'Cable Street' reprinted there, is an acknowledged precursor of *Lud Heat*). In what was largely an anthology of contemporary work, forgotten streams of modernism are acknowledged: the surrealist David Gascoyne joins company with the modernist artist-poet David Jones (who appears as a character in *Landor's Tower*). It is an impressive and personal constellation of poetic energies.

Just as Sinclair's poetry did not cease during the disappointments of the early 1980s, he did not abandon fiction in the years between *Radon Daughters* and *Landor's Tower* (2001). From 1995 to 1997 he published a number of short fictions, which were collected in *Slow Chocolate Autopsy* (1997). Marketed in the fashionable area of the graphic novel, and perhaps testimony to Sinclair's growing status as a cult author after *Lights Out*, in fact only three of the twelve stories feature the graphic work of David McKean. His dark drawings and photocollage overlays perfectly match Sinclair's vision and adorn his new and reprinted books in the early years of the new century.

11

Like *Downriver*, *Slow Chocolate Autopsy* tries to avoid generic pigeonholing in its subtitle, *Incidents from the Notorious Career of Norton, Prisoner of London*. Although intertextually connected to the Petit-Sinclair film *The Falconer*, made in 1996-7, the major intertextual reference lies in the name of the hero, Norton, which is lifted from the first paragraph of Burroughs's *Junky* (1953). He is the man who introduces the Burroughs character, William Lee (the 'author' of the first edition, *Junkie*), to drugs. Sinclair's Norton characteristically 'wants to describe the city' in which he is held captive, 'by logging the contour lines of culture' (*SCA* 51). The writing, which Sinclair has unjustly called 'fairly light and instant' (he describes the project 'throwaway'), is the least lush of Sinclair's career, as though Norton the notetaker has taken over the authorial role, along with that of the narrator's voice, to produce a clipped, sometimes Beckettian, style, an isolated outpost of the Sinclair intratext (*V* 130-31). When Burroughs himself appears in the final story, Sinclair re-narrates the opening lines of *Junky* and replaces 'Norton' with the inoffensive 'Francis'. Writing, in Sinclair's world, as in Burroughs's, is often envisaged as a divinatory act, literally revealing, or influencing, the future. Rewriting, such as this, is to enter chronology and re-order time, to allow Burroughs another life, annulling the connection that tied his work to drugs. Without his name, Norton, the prisoner, is released from the chains of London.

Some critics of *Landor's Tower* (2001) seemed surprised that, Sinclair, who had for many years been thought of as a London writer, bracketed with Ackroyd and Moorcock, should turn his attention to the Ewyas Valley in Wales and to the West Country. But Sinclair (though of distant Scottish heritage) was born in Wales and was educated in Cheltenham, so was no stranger to the territory. As early as *Lud Heat*, Llanthony Abbey, a central location in (and of) *Landor's Tower*, makes its appearance as a node of psychic energy. Indeed, Sinclair has said that he has long planned a series of four 'white chapel' novels, with *White Chappell, Scarlet Tracings* covering the East of Britain, *Landor's Tower* the West. 'The Northern one is set in the Peak District,' Sinclair explains, and the South one is similarly plotted, but both remain unwritten (as of 2006) (*V* 114). Nevertheless, there is a sense in both *Landor's Tower*, and the prose written since the millennium, that inner London had been 'regenerated' (or gentrified) to such an extent that it had lost its gritty charm, its histories no longer secrets. (Even Rodinsky's synagogue is now a 'Spitalfields' heritage centre, a museum of immigration.) The motorways the M4 and the M25 (and the A13 tributary, the locale of *White Goods*) or sixty-mile radius of London's influence, offer imaginative escape routes. By 2003 Sinclair was living for part of the year on the radius, on the south coast. (This is reflected in his novel *Dining on Stones*, which explores both the A13 and the Hastings area. His non-fiction work *Edge of the Orison* (2005), traces the route the insane poet John Clare took from Essex to Northampton. *Sixty Miles Out* is the working title of a planned psychogeographical project to 'follow the coast round, cut up through Cambridge and back down through Oxford, and see what's out there on the rim of where London really loses its identity', while *London: City of Disappearances* (2006) is an edited anthology of pieces on the capital (*V* 136-7).)

Norton the escapee reappears as the anti-hero of *Landor's Tower*. He is failing to write a book on Walter Savage Landor, who, in turn, had failed (like many others) to find utopian simplicity in the borderlands. When Sinclair was asked to pick eight favourite texts for a chapbook series of 'desert island poems', published as *LAND/OR, Poet's Poems* No. 9 in 2002, he summoned Norton as *his* fictional surrogate to select for him, and the result forms an intratextual supplement to the novel, one which underlines the talismanic role of writers in Sinclair's universe, in this case Landor, Vaughan, Brian Catling, Chris Torrance, David Jones, Ed Dorn, J. H. Prynne and Vernon Watkins (all of whom appear in the novel, fictionalized or otherwise).[10] As Sinclair writes elsewhere: 'Poets are never properly incarnated, trapped in their meat bodies. They are too canny to risk everything on a single system of time. It's my conceit to imagine their spirit bodies whirling in a vortex' (*LO* 103). In *Landor's Tower*, the intertextual references build the intratext of the work. Such references construct most of the plot devices from which Norton characteristically tries to escape. While much of the novel covers themes seen elsewhere – the quest for rare texts by a familiar band of book dealers, the attempt to unravel political conspiracy theories, around the Jeremy Thorpe case or around mysterious deaths at the government spy centre in Cheltenham – the last section, 'Resurrection and Immortality', brings a new elegiac tone to the intratext.

Sinclair himself, in a note appended to *London Orbital*, his huge non-fiction volume of 2002, about the M25 motorway, acknowledges a tighter intratextual cluster constellated by four of his books, two of which, *Rodinsky's Room* and *Dark Lanthorns*, I have already discussed; these are joined by *Sorry Meniscus (Excursions to the Millennium Dome)* and the volume of film criticism *Crash* (both 1999). 'Sorry Meniscus' is just one of the multiple epithets Sinclair reserves for the Millennium Dome. The siting on a carcinogenic landfill of the Labour government's 'vision thing' (which it uneasily inherited from the Conservatives who finally left power in 1997), the utter ideological vacuity of its content (it has no theme other than 'Time', the Millennium which it was built to celebrate), along with the squalor and disaffection that surround this charmed circle, as well as the huge sums of money sunk into this heavily marketed 'Experience', were well known when he was writing. Indeed, when Sinclair asks, 'Wouldn't it be more of a challenge to find something positive to say about a construction that was hated by two-thirds of the population?' he reveals his discomfort in offering, for once, the national consensual opinion (*SM* 90). But the sheer verve of his vitriol carries the reader through. When that earlier ambulatory documentarist William Cobbett, in 1822, had first laid eyes on the Royal Pavilion at Brighton, an analogous materialization of pomposity and emptiness, he figured the odious Royal 'Kremlin' as a vegetable box with turnips at the centre and each corner.[11] Sinclair's nearest epithet to Cobbett's, 'a heap of icing sugar with twelve match-ends stuck in it' (*SM* 64), prepares the reader for more politicized 'visions': it is 'Disneyland on message' (*SM* 74); it is 'a bald skull stretched to its limits to accommodate anyone prepared to kick in the necessary millions for a trade stand' (*SM* 82).

Sinclair's *Crash* operates via a series of comparisons, the most pronounced being between the cinematic adaptor and the originator of the novel *Crash*, as expressed in Sinclair's careful, if inelegant, subtitle for the book: *David Cronenberg's Post-mortem on J. G. Ballard's 'Trajectory of Fate'*. Ballard encapsulates the 'death of affect' in his scrupulously deadpan pornographic

14

novel, his swansong to the 1960s, published in 1973 (C 57). Its 'nexus of sex, love, eroticism and death' defines a certain kind of postmodern being (C 80), whereas Cronenberg's 1996 film celebrates a later postmodern condition, the 'Post surveillance anti-drama. The death of excitement', a condition more millennial than the Dome (C 57). For Sinclair, the film's elegant stylization works to 'dilute excitement', (C 69) deflecting the relentless pornography of the original, but this ultimately 'depoliticizes Ballard's frenzied satire' (C 122). Cronenberg also decontextualizes the action from the edge-lands of London to an anonymous Toronto. Despite its having been commissioned by the British Film Institute, the book focuses upon 'a bibliography of Ballard's associations', such as earlier attempts to film the book, including one by Chris Petit, who operates as a contrary (British) spirit to (Canadian) Cronenberg (C 121). Ballard's 'trajectory of fate', inaugurated by his novel of sexualized auto-death, leads from the fiction to the 'real' deaths that are mediated and fictionalized anew by the media, particularly the fatal car crash of Princess Diana in 1997 (C 106). If this sounds like a Sinclair plot, it is one with which Ballard (in Sinclair's interview with him here) colludes. Sinclair knowingly uses his study to nominate Ballard as his avatar, mingling their bibliographies of associations. Indeed, the question he asks of Ballard's work, whether 'the purpose of Ballard's art is to counter a general paralysis of the emotions with metaphors of heat, or whether the author uses his skills to bring about the condition that he fears the most', is one that can be pertinently framed about Sinclair's own projects (C 10).

London Orbital attempts to counter what Sinclair most fears. Its conceit is that to walk the M25, anti-clockwise, as though in order to drive time backwards, will annihilate the Millennium Dome that it encircles (LO 1). If this reads like a parody of the careful pentangular mappings of Lud Heat, in a sense it is, for Sinclair confesses, in a telling use of the passive, that 'it had once been possible to imagine' energy-lines stretching between Hawksmoor churches, but now such patternings present ambivalent hypotheses for discovery (LO 31). The reappearance of Renchi Bicknell – who had been a player in The Kodak Mantra Diaries as well as a model for the itinerant character Rhab Adnam in the fiction – as Sinclair's fellow walker, means that

Sinclair can conveniently project any residual New Age speculations and conspiracy theories onto his friend, the artist celebrant of ley line walking.

Sinclair's predilection – like Rodinsky's – for drawing divinatory lines on maps, in part, dictates his approach towards cultural formation. *Lud Heat*'s willed ley lines generate a wealth of supposedly occult materials for Sinclair to carefully counterpoint with local realist accounts. As *Lights Out*'s walks across London are partly quests for the 'reforgotten' cultural workers of the capital, the circumnavigation of the M25 has not just the disappearance of the Dome as its aim, but the re-appearance of artists it finds along its route, such as the impoverished visionary poet Bill Griffiths in his houseboat at Uxbridge, or the late Barry MacSweeney, who is presented as a modern 'ranter'. Sinclair trudges the sites of the English Revolution and asks

> Was it legitimate to read that decade of samizdat publication (1965-75), poetry wars, readings above pubs or in disestablished chapels, as in any way analogous to the outpourings of the Dissenters (Levellers, Diggers, Ranters) in the years of the English Civil War ... ? (*LO* 186)

Such legitimacy he claims derives from the connections he makes between the poets, between eras, and – crucially – between places (Uxbridge and the Diggers' St George's Hill are both visited).

While I have emphasized the literary over the artistic and counter-cultural, I believe this ley lining of culture – Sinclair 'inscribing his own mental biro-lines on the tarmac, and then excavating and linking up the marked spots', as Barry puts it – is the unifying activity of his intratextual work, in its multiple intertextuality.[12] However, those wishing to create an exclusively avant-garde 'tradition' will be disappointed to discover the environs of Churchill as well as Ballard's bolthole en route in *London Orbital*. The lines Sinclair draws explicitly complicate or refute existing lines of 'influence'; they scribble over the maps of affiliations and allegiances, official and unofficial. They delete as well as connect.

Landor's Tower evokes the central metaphor for these eclectic acts of linkage. Alfred Watkins's theory of the ley line as outlined in his 1925 book *The Old Straight Track* was popular in the 1970s when Sinclair appropriated its method to the Hawksmoor churches. Watkins argues that many of the ancient sites of England and Wales – Stonehenge would be the most famous of these – are aligned with one another in a network of straight lines of communication called ley lines, that are also aligned with the movement of the sun. Watkins's evidence, however dubious, is archaeological, and is largely presented in the form of maps with the straight tracks drawn upon them. Another genius of the borderlands, Watkins enjoys one of Sinclair's set historical pieces in *Landor's Tower*; his description of the invention of ley lines is crucial to understanding Sinclair's psychogeographical and literary politics. Watkins's 'original revelation', is that 'everything connects and, in making those connections, streams of energy are activated' (*LT* 2).

The poetics of modernist juxtaposition have been approvingly evoked, and utilized, by Sinclair: 'Multi-voiced, lyric seizures countered by drifts of unadorned fact, naked source material spliced into domesticated trivia, anecdotes, borrowings, found footage' (*LT* 31). Norton's inventory in *Landor's Tower* could be describing a work like Ezra Pound's *Cantos* (or even Sinclair's own collage *Lud Heat*). In Pound's technique of imagist juxtaposition and in the ideogrammic method of the *Cantos* may be found a literary equivalent of the ley line. Pound states that the juxtaposition of elements without syntactic linkage, by simple contiguous arrangement (if you like, by drawing a line between them) creates new combinations. However, the basis for this emerged from philology as suspect as Watkins's archaeology. The alignment of the four Chinese ideograms for 'rose', 'iron rust', 'cherry' and 'flamingo', Pound attempts to demonstrate, combine to create the single ideogram for 'red'.[13] New meaning, like montage in film, is constructed from the juxtaposition of previously discrete concrete elements.

Sinclair's cultural criticism operates on the principle that 'the official map of the culture, at any time, would always fail to include vital features. Too many good writers are left out of the canon' (*RR* 139). If the cultural explorer cannot trust the cultural mappings, whether the bibliographies of the literary canon, or *The Shell Book of Walks*, whose aim is to induce bucolic amnesia ('These are strolls for the visually impaired, guided tours with checklists'), the only way to establish a working map is empirically, to walk out into the culture (literally, in Sinclair's case) and gather what the walking reveals, to go beyond the official map to find the cultural operators who are off the radar, either because the radar is faulty, or because the cultural mandarins are lazy and dismissive (*LO* 305). The bare narratives of the walks in *London Orbital* (and in *Lights Out*) become bejewelled with significance, and spark with potential cultural connections, like Pound's ideogrammic nodes, dotted ley lines for the reader to follow outwards. If enough connecting lines are ruled across what the sociologist Pierre Bourdieu calls the field of literary and cultural production, in his own spatial metaphor, if the work can make *connections* between these vital nodes of local or repressed cultural activity, then the ghostly template of an alternative culture may be made visible, one that might (if only for Sinclair) negate the dominant world of the literary hack and the culturally validated poet.[14]

Pound's characteristic method was to draw the elements *into* the energy which was the vortex of the poet's mind. In partial acknowledgement of this, Sinclair's poetry anthology, *Conductors of Chaos*, suggests, by its very title, that writers are both *not only* imperfect orchestrators but transmit elements of chaos, rather than order; they stand like the stones between which the ley line enthusiast tracks patterned energies.

This model of Sinclair's cultural politics, deriving as it does from his earliest poetic practice, reveals a brave but risky strategy. Like all empiricism it is the slave of what is discoverable, and what Sinclair finds first are his artist-friends and immediate associates. Through them – Catling dragging him to see Aaron Williamson perform, for example – he discovers other connections, but he risks mythologizing these characters, and himself, as easily in non-fiction as in fiction. When the connections are forced – Rodinsky pushed hard against Pinter – the results are wilful, even desperate. For Sinclair, though, there can be no alternative method; the risks of being wrong are outweighed by the almost utopian connectivity of the imagination, a notion perhaps learned from Ginsberg in those seminal conversations of 1967. Making the future in this way is the corollary of Ginsberg's contention that 'the old MEANS of manufacturing history are called into question' (*KMD* n.p., quoted in *DS* 360).

London Orbital encodes this sense of building a community

around itself at localized levels too. Sinclair dwells on the characters and histories of his fellow walkers, who range from ex-pop star Bill Drummond, who is most famous for burning a million 'quid', to the Cambridge freelance writer and scholar Kevin Jackson (who was also Sinclair's interlocutor in the book-length interview of *The Verbals*, published in 2003). *London Orbital*'s 2002 edition is lavishly illustrated by both David McKean and Renchi Bicknell. Its publication coincided with the broadcast on Channel 4 of an M25 'road movie' made with Chris Petit, also called *London Orbital*. Mainly shot through a slightly opaque windscreen, the film's theme is ultimately the boredom of driving the circular road, and J. G. Ballard appears as a talking head to remind the viewer of the danger of the diffusion of a rootless 'airport culture' throughout Britain (C 84). The gesture of the 1995 Albert Hall event was refined; at the Barbican in 2002, Sinclair curated an evening programme of extreme artistic juxtaposition. (Other events organized by Sinclair range from the 1991 exhibition 'The Shamanism of Intent' at the Goldmark Gallery in Uppingham, to the week of readings that he helped Paul Smith to organize at the Bridewell Theatre, as a platform for Litvinoff, Petit, Raymond and John Healy.) At the Barbican *London Orbital* celebration, Petit's film was shown alongside a performance of Jimmy Cauty's music, using roadside lights as strobes; 'money burning moralist' Bill Drummond and 'former Hell's Angel and present Anglo-Saxon scholar' Bill Griffiths shared a platform, although Drummond read and Griffiths played Bartok.[15] Comedian Ken Campbell delivered a monologue on ventriloquism, while Catling 'whipped out his heart and entrails from deep inside his tuxedo before consuming with much relish, more blood and gore than a B-movie'.[16] If the pattern of the energies configured, and described here by Sinclair, seems eccentric rather than eclectic, random rather than canon-forming, that is testimony to the risk at the heart of the project, its sceptical generosity, its (almost) utopian optimism. The intratext is not just a body of work; it is a model for culture that, as soon as it is proposed, disestablishes itself. To borrow from a title of Peter Ackroyd, Sinclair's works approximate 'notes for a new culture'.

Such a manner of cultural assemblage takes this study some way from its primary focus upon 'writing', and, if I now draw back to consider literary style, it is only to ultimately approach Sinclair's cultural politics from another angle. If 'anyone who cares about English prose cares about Iain Sinclair, a demented magus of the sentence', then it is important to say why.[17] James Wood, who takes this view, explains:

> So purely is he a stylist that he returns prose to a state of decadence: that is to say, one can find Sinclair's mind limited, his leftish politics babyish, his taste for pulp writing tiresome, his occultism untrue, and forgive all of this because the prose, gorgeously amoral, is stronger than the world it inhabits. It consumes the world it inhabits.[18]

Prose – both in fiction and non-fiction – is thus figured as an admirable parasite or cancer, glitteringly destructive of its subject matter (which is dismissed anyway). In this formulation, Sinclair's dementia leaves nothing but the magic of his style, a linguistic Alzheimers of blanked-out content.

To reject this view is not to say that there are no questions that may be raised about Sinclair's politics or his occultism, but neither is it to state that there is nothing more to be said about Sinclair's style. Indeed, one of the first things professional commentators note about Sinclair is the satirical brilliance of his epithets, which seem destined for dictionaries of quotation. Almost the second thing seems to be the identification of where this wit seems forced, the metaphors lacking in judgement, taste or tact. Henry Hitchings inventorizes the successes and failures of *Landor's Tower*:

> His metaphors bristle with malicious intent. One character has eyebrows like 'curls of unlit gunpowder'; another appears to have been 'carved from suet'; a late breakfast comprises 'devilled kidneys and a 'necklace of poached eggs'.... Some of the imagery misfires. Can one really claim that the McDonald's logo looks 'spiky'? And what are we to make of the suggestion that a frightened character 'had the air of an abortionist fleeing from a house case that had gone badly wrong'?[19]

The ambivalence felt by even his admirers derives from the level of risk Sinclair takes with metaphors. Perhaps he is at his most successful when he is suggestive and comic, as when Joblard's exhilaration at being in danger manifests itself: 'He unzipped a Jacobean gash of teeth' (*DR* 364). One stylistic trait has captured a good deal of attention: 'He's over-fond of sentences with no verbs – a stylistic ploy that fits his rapture-of-the-gaze' point of

20

view, as Simon Reynolds has it.[20] Sometimes this takes the form
of compounded serial epithets, such as those used to describe the
Millennium Dome, cited earlier. One source for this is the
paratactic phrasal movement of his free-verse poems, which
derives from an American modernist aesthetic of juxtaposition,
and which Sinclair translates directly into prose. Another is the
commercially dictated economy that Sinclair so admires in the
work of pulp writers. (It is not clear why these writers are
automatically 'tiresome', as Wood contends; Sinclair has spoken of
the 'mediumistic element' that one finds in the work of some of the
'hack' writers that 'is so psychotic that it's beyond genre' (*V* 103).)
While Hitchings admits that the prose 'is incandescent, and the
sentences teem with data – names and arcane observations sprout
with every clause' – he finds this dense mixture 'at times
obstructive; many of the allusions are painfully obscure'.[21]

This is a feeling shared by a fictional editor in *Downriver*, who
is represented purely by the marginalia he deposits upon the
manuscript of 'Sinclair':

> 'The man who had shot, and lost, the definitive Minton. ' 'WHAT IS
> THIS?' screamed [the editor's] reasonable pencil. *What* is this? As if he
> suspected it (Minton) of being some species of effete English
> porcelain. Should I have provided a footnote on the Soho Scene in
> the 1940s and 1950s, on John Deakin the photographer, on John
> Minton...? (*DR* 352)

If Sinclair's work is an evolving intratext, as I contend, then the
prose of *Lights Out* offers the footnotes to these intertextual
references, but that is not the main point here. The question the
'Sinclair' of the fiction asks, with some exasperation – 'Which
names, if any, *would* have been acceptable? – points again to his
practice of constellating a provisional culture of the 'reforgotten', as well as to cultural practices and practitioners who
remain 'arcane' and 'obscure' (*DR* 352). (Deakin the photographer and Minton the painter were once well known, but are
not as far off the map as some of Sinclair's discoveries.) The
question is not so much that references such as these slow the
reading pace for some ideal reader. It is 'painful' for the
assumed official cartographers of culture to face a terrifying *terra
incognita*. For Sinclair's work to be essential to 'English prose'
(and poetry) it is necessary to take on board its cultural

21

presumptions, whatever the intertextual and intratextual difficulties. Rather than a question of ignoring or forgiving his
content, it is one of reading it knowingly and critically.

*

Dining on Stones, published in 2004 by Hamish Hamilton and
Penguin – a significant change of publisher for Sinclair – is his
most postmodern novel. Written in sections that carry the
paratextual device of fake authors and title pages, as well as two
'manuscripts' by Marina Fountain (a typical self-conscious use of
a place name for a character by Sinclair), the text is sprinkled
with photographs of South America purporting to be from
Norton's ancestor's Kodak. On the other hand, the writing –
short paragraphs building up to short chapters – is less ornate,
less given to baroque constructions, more like his non-fiction
style, although it is still highly, even hyperactively, allusive.

The gothic prop of the doppelgänger is enacted in the
bifurcation of Norton's character, as a reflection of Sinclair's own
division of labour, into Andy, the 'one who put the hack into
Hackney' (*DS* 286), the documentary 'urban topographer' (*DS*
374), and A. M. Norton, who is the 'fabulist', removed to the
Hastings area on the Sussex coast (*DS* 374). Each is haunted by the
other, suspecting him of secretly writing his works. The mysterious
Fountain also provides two parallel narratives, the first of which,
'Grays', was originally published in *White Goods*. A stunningly
powerful tale that enacts a ritual killing where the scapegoat takes
on the identity (as well as, quite creepily, the *hands*) of the killer,
this is another of the many doublings of the novel. The 'twin quests
of art and murder' (*DS* 340) are enacted in the 'twin tales' of the
Nortons (*DS* 364), which itself reflects the imagined 'composite
landscape (leading to composite time)' of the two principal
locations (*DS* 351). A superimposed film in a camera suggests that
doubleness is implicit in all acts of perception. When the two
Nortons meet at a spectral motel, face to face in a mirror, one
launches the other through it, to disappear into its double world.
The central Ballardian setting of the roadside motel – one even
boasts a book-dispenser (containing Ballard's fictions) – is an
appropriate postmodern atmosphere-neutral non-place where
'fiction and documentary cohabit' (*DS* 132).

A picaresque adventure to kidnap entertainer Max Bygraves

(they actually pick up the drug dealer Howard Marks, who had previously made guest appearances in both Sinclair's fiction and documentary) leads to the death of the Hackney Norton, which affords the narrational 'I', if not escape, then the opportunity to continue the narrative: 'Norton's third mind had broken cover' (*DS* 370). The characters who follow the Hackney Norton down the A13 (a quest along the eventful tributary of the M25) do escape from the narrative. However, Norton's re-integration leads him to an erotic liaison with the mysterious Fountain, who reveals that 'her' fictions in the book (and the works of the 'other' Norton) are in fact pastiches drawn from his own abandoned fragments. In a plot full of improbabilities the revelation that she is in fact the first of his two ex-wives – another thematic doubling – seems not unreasonable. The book recurrently exposes the mechanisms whereby individuals are represented, either by the act of being fictionalized or by the media. Though this is a staple of postmodernist deconstruction, the crucial representation, as often in Sinclair, is of an event not yet enacted, in this case the death of 'Norton'. Fiction is simply fact waiting to happen, and it is the writer's responsibility to write the narrative away from calamity, which the fabulist Norton manages.

However, the postmodernity of the novel is not inflected by Sinclair's customary occult paranoia (although in a tale with patterns of doubling, paranoia is an unavoidable part of its texture). Norton realizes that the doppelgänger is no 'fetch' but merely an effect of textuality, is 'a grammatical error – he for I' (*DS* 357). 'If they find themselves in the same room, at the same time, the world tilts on its axis,' the novel comments, but it is a vast intertextual world that 'tilts', with the work of Essex-based Joseph Conrad as its 'axis' (*DS* 368). Whereas *Downriver* had consciously used *Heart of Darkness* as its fictional double, here that role is taken by *Nostromo*. Norton flirts quite consciously with the notion that he is a 'mirror-world' parallel for the detached semi-outlaw of Conrad's novel (*DS* 422). Conrad and the ancestral Norton are also twinned, as it were, both 'explorers' of South America, and both suffering financial losses (in Conrad's case both in the fiction and in life). Financial loss haunts both books, and throughout *Dining on Stones* there are negative references to property investment. The margins of

23

Sinclair's London have reached Hastings because of soaring housing costs (a 'boom', if one is a beneficiary), while the 'Thames Gateway' of the A13 promises 'regeneration' on the inner margins of the expanding capital. The features of a number of Sinclair's projects are folded into *Dining on Stones*, thus ensuring its place in the expanding intratext as another 'book-length footnote to his other books'.[22]

1

Poetry: The Hard Stuff. The Toffee of the Universe

The title of Sinclair's first important work, *Lud Heat* (1975), which juxtaposes poems with expository prose, is itself an exemplary juxtaposition. Lud was the mythological king of Britain who is supposedly buried beneath London's Ludgate, and whose name is one of the etymological contenders for the place-name of the capital. Heat is a term used throughout Sinclair's intratext to denote energy, malign or benign, often associated with certain places, and persisting through time. Early in *Lud Heat*, talismanic poets are imagined as 'a sequence of heated incisions through the membranous time-layer' (*LHSB* 16). Place, for Sinclair, as Rachel Potter states, 'is understood as a continuum within history which withholds and determines the particular memories and lore to which it has borne witness'.[1] That *Lud Heat* is subtitled 'a book of the dead hamlets' should not obscure the fact that death does not imply inertia, but potential. *Lud Heat* is identified as 'The Muck Rake Book One'. The allusion operates through the epigraph to the book, from Bunyan's *Pilgrim's Progress*, wherein the pilgrim, 'who could look no way but downward', cries, 'Oh, deliver me from this muck-rake' (*LHSB* 9). At a literal level this points to the fact that *Lud Heat* records Sinclair's period as a grass cutter and gardener for Tower Hamlets Council in 1974, but it also alerts the reader to the existential questioning of the book that results from being both rooted in and held captive by 'place', its heat, and its inescapable 'lore'.

The book's process of composition seems to have arisen out of journals, in which both dreams and reality are meticulously recorded; some of these find their way into the finished book.

25

'An invasion of white rats, scuttling over the steps of a double ziggurat' (*LHSB* 41), matches the precision of his daytime perceptions: 'The white of horse-chestnut candles' (*LHSB* 41). However, Sinclair is no Hopkins looking for the inscape of nature. Textual quiddity comes from chat with his mostly Irish Catholic workmates as they discuss their negative reactions to the death of Princess Anne's horse or the visit of Cardinal Heenan to the East End. The thirty-five poems of the book first appear as extensions of this journal, a poem a day. Barely punctuated, using space and the ampersand to punctuate both meaning and pace, the poems' sentence-phrases hang on the line, their enjambement often at the ends of phrases, leaving an appropriately notational flavour. The first poem begins *in medias res* with an awareness of its potentialities and processes:

> sits
> the coat of darkness, wondering
> if he would ever write it
>
> (*LHSB* 41)

The poems overhear the things of the world, in this case a television, with painful intensity:

> in another room the electric serial
> loud & raw
> has taken something from his eye
>
> (*LHSB* 42)

The self, presented in the third person, is threatened, is still looking downward, but accepts the powers around it. The first poem ends:

> these are the summer words
> & if he works
> it is not all because he has to
> face down
> along the curve of falling energies
> there is nothing more
> or less
> than to become unconscious
>
> to hood the day's falcon
>
> (*LHSB* 42)

26

This extraordinary final image suggests that the essence of daytime consciousness is a fierce predatory gaze that must be actively extinguished. Later the poems rise to generalities and the first-person plural to express their sense of human absorption in, and the lack of escape from, cyclical routine.

> we come out of the cycle of pains
> > or
> the pains become by repetition pleasurable
> are worn down
> > & go into the butter
> of a fat new moon

> > > > (*LHSB* 88)

The passive awareness of uneasy harmony both in consciousness ('dreams are sleek now filled/ with pasturing doubts', *LHSB* 88–9), and in material reality ('the sofas are human/ & enclose every vertebral ache', *LHSB* 89) lends a certain grace to these poems unique in Sinclair's work, the confirmation of personal happiness that strives, in the words of another poem, to 'construct a more generous sentence' (*LHSB* 94). Brittle theorizing is reserved for the prose essays (which were composed later), but these poems also register unease with their own lyrical compass, a striving towards such analysis. Pleasure and pain are insufficient measures as they absorb one another.

> we loll in the pleasure of it
> until that becomes boring & the eyes
> ache again for images they cannot bear

> > > > (*LHSB* 89)

The poetic inheritance of this work is largely American. While the 'relaxed, meditative free verse' derives from that tradition, more importantly so does its permission that a 'poem' might include prose.[2] It was William Carlos Williams who observed that Pound's *Cantos* 'can include pieces of prose and have them still part of the poem. It is incorporated in a movement of the intelligence which is special, beyond usual thought and action.'[3] Williams sought to emulate this in his own *Paterson* (1948–63), which not only uses assorted prose but, like *Lud Heat*, is intensely concerned with locality; the ragbag approach is arguably well suited to capturing the cluttered physical collage of urban space. Olson's *Maximus Poems* (1950–

70) makes use less of prose as a vehicle, but its tightly scored lines of breath-units (also scored for the eye using the layout devices of the typewriter) were dubbed 'Projective Verse' by Olson in his famous poetics essay of that name. Concerned to keep the rhythms of perception and language open and in harmony, sensitive to each momentary experience by emphasizing writerly process and improvisatory spontaneity, through a mobile free verse line, projective verse was an ideal model for Sinclair's journal-like responses to his quotidian existence. Indeed, Sinclair has admitted that, early in his writing life, Olson 'became the major figure for me' (*V* 38). Additionally, Olson's focus upon topological data dealing with New England's early settlement, which Sinclair experienced as 'a sense of somebody nailing down a sea town and opening it up to the world', suggested that a semi-scholarly attention to place might also yield appropriate aesthetic results (*V* 38).

These examples may have influenced British precursors to *Lud Heat*, one acknowledged by Sinclair, the other not. The unacknowledged is Roy Fisher's late modernist evocation of Birmingham, *City* (1960), with its assemblage of varieties of poetic forms and defamiliarizing prose. The acknowledged precursor is Lee Harwood's *Cable Street* (1964), which focuses upon the same East End territory as *Lud Heat*, juxtaposing slight lyrics and background prose, particularly dealing with radical politics (such as the anti-fascist Battle of Cable Street in 1936). Contemporary to Sinclair's own work, Chris Torrance's *The Magic Door* (of which Sinclair published the first two books in 1975 and 1977), is praised in *Lud Heat* for its 'neat fast descriptions' and its ability to show that 'the dream/ with the observed world is shared', both qualities Sinclair has emulated. (*LHSB* 65) Allen Fisher's *Place* project (1971-9), is – in Sinclair's words, an 'Olsonian epic about South London' – which places Blake at the centre of its inspiration (*V* 73). Like Blake, both Fisher and Sinclair were publishers of their own books, in Sinclair's case, adding maps, drawings and photographs to illustrate the text in its Albion Village Press edition. Part of *Place* offers a reading of *Lud Heat* as a fraternal enterprise, which is still one of the best introductions to the work. Fisher recognizes the need to communicate about the nature of place, and the symbolic interpretation of the built environment.

The necessity to locate, to place ourselves becomes increasingly apparent to people living, as you do Iain, in the throws (sic) of, up against the old walls of a city, when this city – London – is now one borough of 33 held in the name of the Greater Council.[4]

Fisher writes approvingly that 'your concern is energetic and about energy' and that Sinclair is concerned with 'situational fields, lapping overlapping', but he sceptically employs a qualifying set of inverted commas when he observes that 'it is from … buildings that the energies of the area are – I was going to say, "generated"'.[5]

Fisher has in mind the theory contained in the essay with which *Lud Heat* opens, 'Nicholas Hawksmoor, his churches'. The architect Hawksmoor, who designed and built London churches in the early eighteenth century after the devastation of the Great Fire of London, is represented as a man who could read the metropolis he found, and, more importantly, who could 'rewrite the city' in a frenzied, barely conscious urge (*LHSB* 14), with 'risky quotations' from architectural history (*LHSB* 14); 'It is possible to imagine that he did work a code into the buildings' (*LHSB* 17). Even the modern standard work on Hawksmoor confesses, 'The strangeness … of many of Hawksmoor's formal devices, has found recognition in the present century's exploration of the subconscious.'[6] The guiding conceit of Sinclair's essay is expressed in the form of a map of London; lines are superimposed upon it in the shape of two pentagrams, rather like Alfred Watkins's ley lines, supposedly demonstrating that Hawksmoor's six churches – he had a hand in a further three – were deliberately aligned with one another for occult signification. What Sinclair attempts in the essay, with its strategic cod academic tone, is analogous to what he accuses Hawksmoor of achieving: quotations are piled on, associated, encoded and presented as 'evidence'. Writers – Yeats, Milton, Blake, Defoe, Bunyan, Keats – are nodes of 'heat' spread around the pattern, 'generated', as Fisher almost cannot bear to say, by the configuration of the buildings. We are promised 'only a fraction of the possible relations' (*LHSB* 16). Hawksmoor's architectural quotations include Egyptian symbols and pyramids, and these assume the darker aspects of the patterning: sun obelisks (more heat) point the reader to invisible plague pits and murder sites, emphasizing the 'unacknowledged magnetism and control-power, built-in code force of these places' (*LHSB* 21). The Jack the Ripper murders of 1888, the Ratcliffe Highway Murders of 1811 (which De Quincey had famously taken a cool look at in his essay 'Murder Considered as One of the Fine Arts' (1827)), and the contemporaneous murder of Abraham Cohen in 1974, had all occurred within the influence lines of these churches, almost literally on their doorsteps. More speculative accounts, that Hawksmoor planned an unrealized basilica after the Primitive Christians on what would become the site of the Carpenters Arms, which was the Kray twins' gangland head-quarters, stretches the threads of the web almost to breaking point. St Anne's Limehouse, which is identified with a mortuary temple, becomes particularly important, with its pyramid (around which, one may read in other sections of the book, Sinclair mundanely mows the grass and against which he 'risks' leaning while he eats his sandwiches). Sinclair himself suffers sunstroke working this patch – the Scorpion god Selkis is invoked by this time – and it is no surprise to learn that 'St Anne's was gutted by fire on the morning of Good Friday, April 6, 1850. Vernal Equinox, time of occult threat' (*LHSB* 37).

While Sinclair is careful to emphasize that his quotations act only as provisional confirmation of one another, of patterns of unacknowledged repetition, the reader is marshalled by a relentless rhetoric of assimilation and connection to believe that these sites are indeed funnels of power for the gods, diffusing their influence through the 'heat' of poets, yet emerging in a violent and violating form in negative acts of murder. Murder, far from being one of the fine arts, is a sacrificial act of purification. The possibility that the family of Abraham Cohen, for example, might not have appreciated this conclusion, should they have read the essay, gives pause for thought. Peter Barry recognizes the danger: 'This overdetermined universe would quickly become unbearably claustrophobic, and perhaps ulti-mately silly, in the hands of any other writer.'[7] It provided a good enough thesis for Peter Ackroyd to run with in *Hawksmoor*, but that was a work of fiction and Sinclair's essay – unless it is read like one of Borges's meticulous inventions – is not. Allen Fisher's scepticism about this overdetermination remains as a powerful corrective. Barry also argues that, despite the mode of argument and its problematics in terms of 'truth' and 'fiction', there is something 'common' to the urban experience in Sinclair's 'mapping out danger points'; he explains, 'The mapping reclaims the city, recuperates its mean, chartered streets, and fits them into an ordered, frightening, preconception'.[8] Once again, Sinclair's actions seem close to that of his invented Hawksmoor, 're-writing' the heat of Lud's territory, as well as to the experience of the ordinary urban dweller.

The finding of equivalences becomes the focus of other prose essays that intersect the poems and journals. The essays on viewing the films of the American experimentalist Stan Brakhage and the sculpture of his friend Brian Catling locate a similar 'autoptic instinct' in the artists' practices (*LHSB* 78). While Brakhage is literally filming an autopsy – 'meaning "the act of seeing with one's own eyes", from the Greek' (*LHSB* 54) – Catling 'serves the Necropolis. Objects are made in fear & expectation of death. In photographs we see the wooden pyramid that is so close to the Limehouse pyramid, & was made in advance of the first sight of it: intentional, willed, prevision' (*LHSB* 84). Art is an energized, unacknowledged intensifier of circumstance and the lore of place; the artist is a variety of shaman, simultaneously blessed and cursed with vision. But the narrator of these pieces – culturally sophisticated and self-regarding – is still the character who waters his broad beans after work and records that fact. He writes of his family (and family to come): 'Anna sickens towards the new life/ the frog-bud forcing itself in her womb' (*LHSB* 134). But this is balanced against the recognition that 'death/is every mother's prophecy'; the hot dead of the dead hamlets are always beckoning (*LHSB* 134).

At the centre of these discourses, contending with these patterns of connection, is the 'narrator'. Sinclair is here recognizing the problematics of autobiographical representation, but also capturing a sense of the discontinuous self that the artist-shaman must assume. He wonders 'when I am/ "not quite myself"/ what (not who)' he is (*LHSB* 50). Egoic dissolution, activated psychosomatically by the Limehouse contagion of sunstroke (and by hay-fevers, upon which he theorizes), is addressed in the essay 'In the Surgery of the Sun':

> As the ego breaks I am host to another being, who pushes through & not with the pink tenderness of new skin – but with old flesh, hard

as wood. The earlier 'I-do-not-know-who-I-am' virus is confirmed, as this terminal caricature eases out of my face. (*LHSB* 109–10)

Host is held hostage by the parasite. Sinclair appears here as Robert Louis Stevenson's Jekyll, fully aware that Hyde is bursting through. Indeed, Stevenson is quoted: 'As for myself I cannot believe fully in my own existence ... the weather is threatening' (*LHSB* 50). At times there is a more beneficent sense of diminished selfhood, of a sinking of self in perception, almost a Zen Buddhist approach to the process; characteristically, this appears in the poems:

> subdue all ego
> (& rigorous eye)
> into the unmarked
> morning quality of autumn light

(LHSB 124)

To break the patterns that the text builds up, to approach something like this 'unmarked' experience, the energy must be annulled or countered. On a literal level, the 'narrator' has to leave his summer employment. On another level, he must return to the map and locate an 'oracle', on the outer point of London. He must then run to the oracle and return; a state of 'total body exhaustion' is ordained (*LHSB* 138). That the oracle turns out to be a urinous machine-gun bunker in the Lea Valley seems not to matter at this stage of Sinclair's career. Later, he would allow irony to undercut the cosmic patterning. It is, however, a ritual he feels impelled to enact, as, later, Sinclair is drawn in his documentary to become a stalker of predetermined routes. This run even prefigures his need to circumnavigate the M25, as a ritual of annihilation, in *London Orbital*. But his final state is a kind of Keatsian negative capability before the energies he invokes, an imperturbable emptiness rather than oracular fulfilment. Like the artist figure in Blake's *Jerusalem*, Los, whose healing pilgrimage across London matches his own, he annihilates selfhood. 'He knows nothing of the precisions & mechanics & movements & meanings here either. An ignorant man, ground-held, muddy in motive – he jogs back the way he came' (*LHSB* 134).

The route back includes a crossing of the Suicide Bridge, where the Kray gang divested itself of incriminating evidence;

this becomes the dark centre of the next book of the Sinclair triad, which takes the bridge's grim name as its title. *Suicide Bridge* (1979) avoids the diaristic, personal approach of *Lud Heat* altogether. Subtitled both 'a book of the furies' and 'a mythology of the South & East', this alerts the reader to the changes of focus. The localized 'muck-rake' has been abandoned for a wider topological range and a turn to narrative. The text is dated 1973–8; it overlaps with *Lud Heat* rather than succeeds it. Whereas *Lud Heat* was largely passive in the face of the energies and myths it envisioned, *Suicide Bridge* is active in attempting to define and manipulate or subvert myth and, whatever the difficulties, to manufacture its own furies. This is demonstrated in *Suicide Bridge*'s equivalent of the Hawksmoor introduction, an interleaved double-essay entitled 'Intimate Associations: Myth and Place', with which the book opens. 'Myths are lies,' it states (*LHSB* 147); they emerge 'in the hands of men wanting to maintain a contact with the previous, with the era of power and high function' (*LHSB* 148). Nostalgia rather than anything approaching religious belief activates the search for validating myths – whether they are ancient or modern, orthodox or invented. They signal lack, rather than the comforts of authority, a failure 'to be on terms with the life-spill of this moment' (*LHSB* 149). They risk the 'vertical energy' of fascism, vertical because the energy appears to dig deep but takes nobody anywhere (*LHSB* 149). That acknowledged – and the essay could be read as a self-criticism of the authorizing myth Sinclair made out of Hawksmoor – this retrogressive impulse can generate power that can be used more positively in the present, to become 'live newsprint' (*LHSB* 149), to emphasize (as Sinclair had in *Lud Heat*, employing similar terms) 'that death is not a period to the heat of man' (*LHSB* 147). This is not a view of death as an ending that gives necessary meaning to life, life as a being-towards-death as the philosopher Heidegger has it, since death may be the beginning of transmogrified narratives. 'Myth is the living breath of place,' Sinclair states (*LHSB* 149), yet 'place' is ultimately 'where you die', not where you are rooted, but where you actively travel towards, in space and time (*LHSB* 153). This nomadic de-territorialization represents the opposite of the Heideggerian concept of place, which the postmodern geographer David Harvey criticizes as 'Place construction ... about the recovery of roots, the recovery of the art of dwelling'.[9] But Harvey's contention that 'to write of the 'power of place' as if places ... possess causal powers', which Sinclair does, 'is to engage in the grossest of fetishisms', serves as a reminder of the originality of Sinclair's theorizing and of its limitations. Harvey's 'definition of place as a social process' has few outlets in this formulation.[10]

William Blake is an earlier example of a poet who made an intimate association between mythic characters and place-names, and Sinclair freely adapts elements from *Jerusalem, Emanation of the Giant Albion* (1804). Jerusalem, an image of Liberty, is both a place and a mythic character: the city of peace and the divided female part (emanation) of the spirit of England, Albion. Separate from their father in his moral sickness, they objectify Albion's evil feelings in his states of selfish withdrawal and shame at the opening of the poem. Ultimately, they unite in the figure of Hand, the eldest son, who Blake scholar Foster Damon calls an 'executioner'.[11] Their objective is to 'keep the nation blind and asleep'.[12] As Blake puts it, in their

> orbed void of doubt, despair, hunger & thirst & sorrow ...
> The twelve sons of Albion, joined in dark assembly, ...
> Became as three immense wheels, turning upon one another
> Into non-entity, and their thunders hoarse appal the dead
> To murder their own souls, to build a kingdom amongst the
> dead.[13]

Thus they are kinds of suicides, burning their negativity into the soil. Blake assigns each his own cathedral town ('Hand dwelt in Selsey ... Hyle dwelt in Winchester'), topological associations that Sinclair broadly follows, although he appropriates the characters of the Sons of Albion for his own purposes.[14] Sinclair uses nine of Blake's twelve, all of whom were named after real people who had (according to Blake) mistreated him. Thus the three-headed Hand is the Hunt brothers who had criticized Blake's work; Hylé – accented thus – is a Cockney amendment of the name Hayley, that of the patron with whom Blake fell out. The others – Skofeld, Kox, Hutton, Coban, Slade and Kotope, to name only those that Sinclair adapts – are similar graphological modifications of the names of accusers, witnesses and justices, some identifiable, some not, at Blake's treason trial, held in the same year he published *Jerusalem*. Blake's mythology has a mocking and satirical grounding in reality that is often missed, and Sinclair keeps the names but re-allocates personalities, as it were. (It is not until he writes fiction that Sinclair disguises the names of real characters in this Blakean fashion.) Thus Hand and Hyle take on the personae of those presiding geniuses of Suicide Bridge itself, the Kray twins, Ronnie and Reg.

While Blake provides the aliases, Michael Ondaatje and Edward Dorn provide stylistic models in their book-length narrative poems, *The Collected Works of Billy the Kid* (1970) and *Gunslinger* (1968–75). Both deal with the mythology of the Wild West, a curious analogy for East End gangsterism. While *The Collected Works of Billy the Kid* shows how to collage poetry, prose and illustrations, its fullest influence derives from its obsession with the death and posthumous myths (the 'works') of Billy the Kid. *Gunslinger* has been described as a 'long laughing anti-epic of the American Southwest ... a kind of comedy of dogmatism, parodic and even self-parodic', and lends to *Suicide Bridge* its mocking distance.[15]

The 'cosmogony' of Hand and Hyle – the theory or myth of the creation of their universe – uses a parodic recasting of scientific notions of the universe, particularly current work on space-time and black holes by Stephen Hawking, who is quoted ironically in the text. It is from such a hole that the twins emerge, gradually assuming their new names until 'they must be, born again, anchored/ to the fate, the corruption, of his island city' (*LHSB* 159). They develop along what Sinclair calls the 'narrative track' (*LHSB* 167), via a number of mythological associations, to become the embodiment of a dual evil, the 'zygotic drama' of the Kray twins, (*LHSB* 168) located in a specific place, 'washed ashore/ 178 Vallance Road' (*LHSB* 167). This is a key location, the Krays' maternal home, for the 'sons/ dutiful & hating women' (*LHSB* 167). Two other places resound throughout Sinclair's work as totemic sites of unspeakable acts of violence that exemplify the 'corruption' of man: the Blind Beggar pub where Ronnie (Hand) shot George Cornell for calling him a 'poof', and Evering Road, where Reg (Hyle) killed Jack 'the Hat' McVitie for having become troublesome to the gangland community:

> the breadknife goes in below the eye
> opens the stomach

> through the windpipe into the carpet
>
> flesh disposal, ritual feasting
>
> (*LHSB* 169)

It is the ritual nature of this killing that finally defeats them. 'Hand & Hyle: Declining' shows the strangely comic twins suffering psychosomatic symptoms, with 'bolts in the brain' (*LHSB* 192). Even their legendary sartorial elegance militates against them, as it hides neurosis about the body, and the repressed sexual orientation to which Cornell unwisely had made reference.

> Hand's irrational
>   fear of yellow socks
> the mustard optimism
> scrambles up his nerves
>
> (spews fear)
>
> short-circuit emotions
> flagellate his haemorrhoids
>
> always the grey suiting,
> the dark socks,
> coal-blacked shoes & hair,
> polished equally,
> scalp & feet: a horror white
>
> but he did, love & fuck
>   the pigment
> of assorted headless bodies
>
> (*LHSB* 190)

A punctilious necrophile, Hand finally becomes the place he haunts, his body penetrated by its effluents,

> to consult the oracle of the streets
>
> black ooze of buildings
> floods his eye ...
>
> the light even now
> burns through the skin holes ...

fog is pouring from his nose,
Hand is walking death

(*LHSB* 196)

The twins are indeed the instruments of death, but do not pass through the gates of myth themselves. (Readers will have to wait for Sinclair's account of Ron Kray's regal funeral in *Lights Out for the Territory* to see how a very different mythology of the Krays took grip of a community: that of loveable rogues who kept the streets clean of crime.) Hutton, 'Missing Presumed Dead', in the ironical title of one of the poems, is a 'mad samurai taken away, released by 'friends', by Hand & Hyle, as token of their power. Kept in a room at the margin of the City. Driven to the riverside, killed' (*LHSB* 205). He is also associated with emblems of death found on Dartmoor (also the site of the prison he was in): mysterious animal carcases, whose grisly photographs adorn the pages of the Albion Village Press edition, their deaths and places of death doubly recorded. The equation between being *a* stiff, a corpse, and being stiff, sexually erect, yet 'passionless/ beyond arousal', prepares the reader for Hutton's final dissolution, through dismemberment (*LHSB* 220). This act is, ironically, one of erection, as he becomes a virtual monument, a fallen colossus.

> Hutton the stiff one
> revolves through the cement mixer
> > conglomerate
> with flint & gravel, with sand-dredged aggregates
> > tipped,
> > > born into the East Way Flyover ...
> a literal and continuing part of the City
>
> we commute between the vast spread of his thighs

(*LHSB* 221)

Kotope is a Jewish businessman with a love of the occult and connections with the underworld, including Hand and Hyle, and 'Peachey, the hit man', another Son of Albion (*LHSB* 186); he is therefore a 'self-proclaimed Zen Master dishing out sharp lessons' (*LHSB* 182). 'Kotope, in fear, plunges through ancient systems,/ his Rolls Royce Corniche cruises the eastern city' in a pilgrimage that has him hankering after the mystery of the

Cathars, Gurdjieff and even Hand and Hyle's vagital black holes, in an attempt to escape the inevitability of death (*LHSB* 180). In the poem 'Kotope, the Manner of His Dying: Six Arabs on the Doorstep', the assassins 'in flower shirts & synthetic beagling tweed ... carrying bren guns/ Czech armament, howitzer, Mao books', embody everything earthly he fears: Arab terrorism and revolutionary politics. The fleeting moment of his death fragments his attention, dissipates his intelligence, but significantly, like Hand and Hutton, he asserts his sexualized identification with place:

> his will
> erects one final, animal, vision of the city,
> his body its body, flying,
> & is gone

(LHSB 185)

These highly gendered and violent deaths pin the 'heat' of the dead men to their place. Similarly priapic, Slade, in the prose piece 'Slade and the Tyrannicides', navigates by 'the compass of his prick', which is virile enough to deliver a considerable blow to his own body (*LHSB* 200). His 'response to landscape' – he is walking on the sacred territory east of London, towards Waltham Abbey, the burial place of King Harold – is not sacramental, but 'violent: snatching'. (*LHSB* 200) That verb hints at the slang noun for the female genitals, snatch. The deaths of the Sons of Albion bespeak a sexualized obsession with egoic extinction beyond their power; their deaths, often passive, are essentially suicides. When the tyrannicides of the title arrive, they prove to be Hand and Hyle. 'Excess of wisdom has made them mad,' Sinclair comments, revising Blake's proverb 'The road of excess leads to the palace of wisdom' by removing its ambiguity: excess, suggests Blake, may also lead to the wisdom of abstinence.[16] Sinclair spares the details of the attack – 'from car to Slade is frenzy' – but Slade's head is cut off (*LHSB* 204). This directly refers to the murder of minor villain Billy Moseley in September 1974, but may also allude to the condition of Jack the Hat after his murder. Yet the severed head can equally stand for Bran's Head – interred in the White Hills to safeguard Wales – as well as the head of Williams, the man accused of the Radcliffe Highway murders, who was dismembered after he committed suicide. Slade's head, nestling in Hyle's lap, cut off from its phallic power, assumes an unlikely oracular potency.[17]

> It speaks the whole *Cantos* of Pound ... Martian Hymns, the Cabbala, Gregorian chants, death songs of defeated Plains Indians, stock exchange quotations, Presley's first cut for Sun Records, Northumbrian Pipes – everything reduced, squeezed, synthesized to one finite buzz. (*LHSB* 203–4)

This is a vision of culture concentrated and levelled to the point of extinction, an insane excessive intensity that reflects that of Hand and Hyle.

Slade's head follows the furtive public house itinerary that Williams' head supposedly followed, but instead of being lost in its own myth, Slade's rematerializes in a cubicle of a subterranean public convenience in Islington, as did Moseley's slowly defrosting head, six months after his murder. Blake ends *Jerusalem* with the re-invigoration of England, the resurrection of Albion, and the defeat of his Sons; Sinclair ends *Suicide Bridge* with the section 'Beneath Brass, Bone, the Prophecy of Slade, the Fate of England', which echoes Blake's promise of fateful prophecy, but gives the final silent soliloquy to the severed head. 'The episode that is & was Slade he is reluctant to conclude, to close down, until the word, whose ghost he is, has been spoken' (*LHSB* 294). Linguistically sealed, Slade's 'word', his hermetic oracle, embodied only in Sinclair's breathless prose, can have no audience but the dead. 'The Heroes do not want to keep everything as it is – but to make it as it was in Myth Time, which never happened, but which is happening now as they strike the first surrogate blow' (*LHSB* 296). The text itself is this surrogate, as Slade takes upon himself the protection of Britain and proposes to build a gated wall of brass to 'speak out of the corruption of the city' (*LHSB* 296). But this is not the free city of Jerusalem; the close reader of Blake will recognize that brass is the element the tyrannical god Urizen uses to make binding laws. Slade is an ersatz guardian, and prefers 'a kingdom amongst the dead'.[18] As a believer 'in visionary release through action', Slade returns us to Sinclair's assertion of the causal relationship between 'Myth Time' and fascism. While Blake held that 'energy is eternal delight',[19] for Slade 'All energy is war' (*LHSB* 299). While Blake believed that 'without contraries there is no progression',[20] Slade proposes a static resolution: 'opposites united, stitch the flux' (*LHSB* 299). Rebirth results not in the resurrection of Albion, but in a re-entry into cycles of evil and pain.

> the assembled fragments
> join to illude a new world, globe
> of spittle shot into a snake's eye
>
> time is what we cut out of the reptile's belly

(LHSB 300)

Life is imaged as a predatory ripping out of guts; death is what must necessarily ensue. The words of Tony Lambrianou, one of the Kray 'firm' (who appears later in Sinclair's fiction and non-fiction), serve to remind how this scenario literally transpired in the case of one of the Krays' murder victims, Jack the Hat. 'We rolled him gently over. Everything was hanging out of his stomach. His liver fell out, and we scooped it up with a little shovel and burned it on the fire.'[21]

Against the appeal of this vicious mythology, other parts of *Suicide Bridge* – the accounts of the comic antics of the Cambridge academics Skofeld and Kox, who seem equally at home in the worlds of literature, the occult and science; or the account of a walk to locate Coban in the cathedral cities – do not arouse such terror. However, the long speculative essay 'The Horse. The Man. The Talking Head' marshals the manifold conspiratorial myths that accrue to the reclusive existence of millionaire Howard Hughes, who both influenced US presidents and tried to rarefy himself out of the pain of bodily existence, but finally chose 'coded narcosis, dim colour sleep', and collecting his urine in bottles (*LHSB* 243).

In a letter to Sinclair concerning *Suicide Bridge*, the poet Douglas Oliver fears that Sinclair's obsession with the Krays, amongst others, is 'yielding creativity into bad vortices', and is tainted with prurience, or sensationalism (*WCST* 159–60). Unlike *Lud Heat*, where the patterns of ordinary life counterpoint the grand theories, the constructed mythologies of *Suicide Bridge*, such as Slade's prophecy, promise nothing but further evil as an inescapable presence within ordinary life. Oliver poses the problem in neo-Blakean terms: 'Can the poetry effect the

40

resolution of good and evil into the coincidence of contraries?' (*WCST* 160). But the contraries are not ethically neutral, cannot simply balance; Oliver pitches for the 'sovereignty of good', a term of Iris Murdoch (*WCST* 162). Whereas Sinclair's 'phantasms' attempt to prove that 'great evil demands as great a soul as does great good' – a near-quotation from Pascal – Oliver believes evil to be 'small-minded and furious like an atompower release, and ... good to expand "in love"'[22] (*WCST* 161). Sinclair, writing of the Kray funeral in 1995, in *Lights Out for the Territory*, recognizes this smallness when he quotes one of the Twins on the murders of Cornell and McVitie: 'It's because of them that we got put away', and comments: 'A nice piece of sophistry – to blame your victims for making you kill them' (*LOT* 71). Yet this is the predatory attitude that underlines the universe of *Suicide Bridge*; it has no room to consider the notion that 'love/ moves the sun' as its contrary, *Lud Heat*, contends (in words which are themselves echoes of Dante's ecstatic incomprehension before the beneficent cosmic order revealed at the end of the *Divine Comedy*) (*LHSB* 131). The doubt for Sinclair, as he observed of J. G. Ballard's work as late as 1999, is whether, in exposing evil, the writer does not bring about that which he most fears. Oliver also alludes to what the philosopher Hannah Arendt called the banality of evil. Hand's dread of yellow socks hints at the utter lack of sensationalism in real criminal life, but there are few acknowledgements of this in Sinclair's mythic apparatus. Contrast this with the autobiographical account of Lambrianou scooping McVitie's guts with a 'little shovel' quoted above, and one recognizes the banality inherent in that precise detail.

That Oliver's pertinent criticism of *Suicide Bridge* was published as part of Sinclair's next work, the third in the triad, *White Chappell, Scarlet Tracings*, not only demonstrates Sinclair's continuing commitment to the collagist techniques of his two poetry books in his fiction, but also testifies to his generous openness to criticism, and to his prophetic sense that the letter's 'time would come. ... The nerve-ends that Doug's letter touched are still twitching' (*WCST* 165).

2

Mere Fiction
(i.e. it hasn't happened yet)

'If you read Sinclair only for the story, you would hang yourself,' writes Roz Kaveney, acknowledging rather starkly the inadvisability, and the impossibility, of attempting to summarize the plots of Sinclair's fictional narratives, including the three novels I will examine here.[1] It is not so much that the reader does not know what is happening; it is that too much happens. The fiction aspires to the novelistic condition Michael Moorcock calls the 'multiverse', in which, as Sinclair glosses it, 'alternate selves live different lives, simultaneously' (*LT* 105). One reviewer, Nicholas Lezard, conjectured of the first novel I will be examining, *White Chappell, Scarlet Tracings* (1987), that 'the mise-en-scene may be [Peter] Ackroyd's',[2] an intertextual relation I have touched on in the introduction, but, by the time of the second novel *Downriver* (1991), Angela Carter, for one, saw the true allegiance: 'The decisive influence on this grisly dystopia is surely the grand master of all dystopias, William Burroughs.'[3] Burroughs's late trilogy – *Cities of the Red Night* (1981), *The Place of Dead Roads* (1983) and *The Western Lands* (1987) – domesticates the excessive and disruptive processes of the cut-up technique, while retaining his legion of near-mythological characters. Influenced by postmodern masters, such as Borges and Calvino, Burroughs feeds his sensibility, which remains committed to all methods of resisting control, through baroque overlapping and, often unresolved, narratives. His characters are granted the agency to 'experiment with identity'; they pass through time and space to create a dystopian multiverse, in which their mission is to overcome death (*LT* 105).

42

By the time Sinclair was writing the third novel I will examine, *Landor's Tower* (2001), a character with a name lifted from Burroughs's work, Norton, haunts the narrative, in which, as Burroughs was fond of saying, and Sinclair is fonder of paraphrasing, the paranoid is the central figure because he (and the figure is always male for both writers) is the only one who possesses a full account of the conspiratorial world he inhabits; that is, all the possible stories. Since these are fictional worlds, it follows that 'mere fiction' may be defined as that which 'hasn't happened yet', as Sinclair does in his 'Acknowledgements and Confessions' to *Downriver* (*DR* 407). As in Burroughs's work, Sinclair's 'real' characters (often with changed names) populate 'fictional' worlds, and vice versa. One of the characters (in the first two of these novels) is called 'Sinclair' and as Sinclair 'confesses' of his dramatized autobiographical presence: 'I can't go as far as to claim that "this version of history is my own invention"' – the quotation is Ackroyd's disclaimer at the end of *Hawksmoor* – but 'these inventions are versions of my own history'[4] (*DR* 407).

Ultimately, reading Sinclair's fiction is an encounter with possible worlds, parallel worlds, dystopias and utopias, coexisting in the multiverse, without apparent contradiction. Acts of writing are, therefore, explorations in creating something other, as Edith Cadiz, a character in *Downriver*, demonstrates:

> Edith writes, steadily and fast, her account of events that connect with these events; but which are *not* these events, and are *not* an account. She does not describe what has happened. She describes something else, which exists, independently, beyond the confines of this close room. (*DR* 78)

The effect of such writing is ironically to induce re-enactments of events that were not enacted in the first place, and are prophetic of 'occurrences' that may never happen.

> What she had done was to ensure that anyone who read her notes with attention would be led to 're-enact' the sequential prophetic curve that any play has to be. The script was a series of physical properties for a séance that would deliver the event Edith was imagining. (*DR* 114)

When a horror story, Machen's 'The Great God Pan' (1894), is brought into service as a divinatory device in *Landor's Tower,*

Norton poses a question about its power, and comments of its somatic and magical effects, in a manner well beyond the reach of rational literary criticism:

> Such is the power of [the] intricate rhythms that the covert pulses of language mimicked the irregular beat of my heart. What if, in surrendering ourselves to the magic of a text, we enter the dream at such a level that we are unable to break free?' (*LT* 184)

Again, as in Burroughs's work, wilfully to enter a new narrative, as Sinclair's characters do, is not to make a version of history, but is to enact a new history. As Burroughs notes matter-of-factly: 'What writers write happens.'[5] In reading the fiction of Sinclair's intratext, a reader must be prepared for such intertextual leakages into reality, and for autobiographical leakages into fiction, and for the productive aporia of the paradoxes that result, in which one senses the author – in a multiverse himself – both believes and does not believe.

WHITE CHAPPELL, SCARLET TRACINGS

White Chappell, Scarlet Tracings completes the 'triad' begun with the poetry books *Lud Heat* and *Suicide Bridge*, but even in those works of the 1970s there had been pre-figurations of the central obsession of Sinclair's first novel: the fate of 'the five wretched victims of the sociopathic serial killer known as "Jack the Ripper"' in Whitechapel between August and November 1888.[6] The gothic title of *White Chappell, Scarlet Tracings* celebrates the elusive track of blood left by the prostitutes' gruesome dismemberments across the East End of what was, by then, the largest metropolis in the world, of five and a half million people. However, the identity of one of these inhabitants, the 'Ripper', as much as the details of the murders themselves, has been an abiding obsession of what has been called 'Ripperature', the mountains of print upon the subject that have amassed since 1888.[7] Clive Bloom relates its genesis to the rise of the press, which popularized 'Jack'; he has inhabited the twilight zone between reality and fiction ever since, which, it must be remembered, is the very space in which Sinclair's fiction flourishes.

Jack the Ripper is a name for both a necessary fiction and for a fact missing its history. Here fiction and history meet and mutate so that the Ripper can be searched for by 'historians' of crime at the very same moment that he can appear in a Batman comic.[8]

When Bloom notes that 'the Ripper's deeds are ever reworked to remain forever contemporary', he could be describing *White Chappell, Scarlet Tracings*; when he says such deeds are 'curiously emphasized by layers of nostalgia', he is describing the danger of the novel's method, while he recognizes how 'Ripperature' forms 'the facets of a scenario for a script about modernity' that hovers between the contemporary and the nostalgic.[9]

White Chappell, Scarlet Tracings consists of three interwoven narrative strands: a contemporary, 1980s, one; a near-contemporary one, set in the 1970s; and a number of connected Victorian pastiches and set pieces, concerning Ripper suspects and their associates.

The strand set in the 1980s concerns the business transactions of a trio of booksellers (with thinly disguised Blakean misnomers, like Dryfeld or misattributed place names, such as Nicholas Lane), narrated by a Sinclair avatar who appears simply as 'the narrator', as he had in *Lud Heat*. The tone is comic, the action slapstick. They encounter Dickensian-sounding book dealers, such as Mossy Noonmann, and the lower orders of the taxonomy of book buyers, the Outpatients and the Scufflers, as they asset-strip shops across the country, and prepare to sell their vanload of stock at marked-up prices. The narrator, in his customary third person, notes his involvement in 'this tawdry profession: he does not have the spirit, yet, to be proud of these fine and active corruptions' (*WCST* 24). His growing conviction that he is being positioned like the narrator Dr Watson – 'the secret hero who buries his own power in the description of other men's triumphs' (*WCST* 15) – is appropriate because one treasure they find is an apocryphal 'trial copy, or a proof of some kind', of Conan Doyle's first Sherlock Holmes story, *A Study in Scarlet* (1887) (*WCST* 25). It is clearly worth 'Ten to twenty. Grand. Plus', in Nicholas Lane's laconic telegraphese. The group has not only scored; it can identify an addict. The analogy of these predatory dealers with drug pushers suggests a refinement of what Burroughs called the 'algebra of need'.[10] The monomaniac bibliophile J. Leper-Klamm (his name suggests both disease and repression as well as a hint at Kafka's *The Castle*) is a government bureaucrat who collects editions of this (and no other) book, an obsession without which 'he would have been so invisible that he could not have functioned' (*WCST* 88). Klamm is trapped in Nicholas Lane's flat to effect the sale, and the result is immediate. Klamm 'has the grail in his hands, it answers him, his life spills, everything connects. He transubstantiates; he is translated' (*WCST* 100). The text of *A Study in Scarlet* recomposes into an oracular cut up before his eyes: 'Deep in the enemy's country … Nothing but misfortune and disaster … I was struck … shattered the bone' (*WCST* 100–101). But these 'icy intimations' from his intertextual consummation with the book are both confirmed and undercut by the immediate entry of comically classic robbers – 'black stocking masks, rhino faced' – who destroy every object of value in the room and fleece its bookselling occupants (with a certain amount of poetic justice) (*WCST* 101). They 'could have been', the narrator speculates, in words that remind us that this novel is connected to *Suicide Bridge*, 'furies from the ether, consummated out of their own paranoia', but the definite 'well-polished black boots and blue shirts' suggest that they might be corrupt policemen (*WCST* 102). They rip the fabulous document to shreds. 'That tunnel into time was sealed,' comments the narrator (*WCST* 102). Klamm, a false visionary, addicted to the sensation of a single text, an occultism of possession, is annulled. He disappears from the novel.

The second narrative strand, set in the 1970s, concerns the Laurel and Hardy exploits of 'Sinclair' and S. L. Joblard. The latter, based on Sinclair's friend the sculptor Brian Catling, is one of his consistently comic creations. Catling has said of Sinclair's method of characterization, 'He casts people in his notion of their fantasies and then develops them.'[11] The pair share a fantastic obsession with the Whitechapel murders. As in *Lud Heat*, 'the zone was gradually defined, the labyrinth penetrated. It was given limits by the victims of the Ripper' (*WCST* 35). They cultivate the friendship of Mr Eves at the Truman Brewery in Brick Lane, who keeps a record of the murders. They lay out the initials of the victims on cards in order of death; it spells 'MANAC ES CEM JK' (*WCST* 51). Like a tarot pack of the dead, or a Ouija board, they play with the resulting sentence. Characteristically, 'the cold truth of that fiction is between' the two men (*WCST* 51). Do the letters attempt to spell 'maniac'? 'Jack is Come'? The concluding 'JK' is felt to be particularly powerful; like the text of J. Leper-Klamm (an almost JK himself), these letters connect with virtually everything. Chapter 24 ends with a piece of concrete prose constellating various names around a giant JK: John Kennedy, Jack Kerouac, Jekyll the Doctor, as well as the K of Philip K. Dick, Joseph K. from Kafka, and even 'Mistah Kurtz' of Conrad's *Heart of Darkness* (1902). When everything connects like this, the paranoiac indeed possesses truth, but is mad. 'Sinclair' and Joblard apparently know this fact. The pair – enjoying the effects of a cannabis cake – watch a TV documentary featuring one of Ripperature's more enduring speculations. As 'Sinclair' sees a photograph of the Ripper 'suspect', Sir William Gull, he is convinced 'It is the face of Joblard, the orphan. Sir William Gull has stolen the face' (*WCST* 55). As ever, comedy undercuts the horror. Joblard does not witness this 'exchange of wills', for he is vomiting the effect of the cake in the bath (*WCST* 55).

In the following chapter the pair consciously assume the roles of Holmes and Watson (with 'Sinclair' again as Watson).

> 'I think,' said Joblard, indicating with his pipestem a copy of Stephen Knight's book, *Jack the Ripper, The Final Solution*, 'that we have been saved a great deal of donkey work. This scenario is remorselessly argued and … it arrives at the castlist we have already floated.' (*WCST* 57)

The hypothesis that the ersatz Holmes accepts remains only partially developed in the novel. Knight's book, which was published in 1976, argues that, in order to cover up an affair that Eddy, the Duke of Clarence, son of Queen Victoria, had with a doubtful woman of the lower orders, the Masonic Lodges recruited their own to kill the woman (since she had attempted to blackmail the Royal Family). A series of misidentifications of the woman and the fear of a conspiracy among prostitutes, necessitated the sequence of ritual killings. None of this appears in *White Chappell, Scarlet Tracings*, although the 'castlist' of men recruited for the task, remains: Sir William Gull, the foremost surgeon of the day (the victims were disembowelled so swiftly that it was assumed that the Ripper was medically trained);

Netley, the queen's coachman, who was needed to provide the getaway; and, although he is merely called 'the painter' in the novel, Walter Sickert, who was a friend of Prince Eddy (and who did have an obsession with the murders in 'real' life). Knight's book, with its combination of scholarly sources, archival material, interviews with 'witnesses', and a strong sensationalist streak of groundless speculation, is not only a perfect example of 'Ripperature'; it – if unconsciously – places itself on the cusp of fiction and history, which is exactly where Sinclair most potently finds his materials.[12]

Knight's book is too obvious a clue for 'Sinclair' and Joblard in their guise as Watson and Holmes, and they turn psychic literary detectives. In his introduction to Conan Doyle's *A Study in Scarlet* (2001), Sinclair states the effects on him of the 'twofold nature' of Conan Doyle's book:

> First, the unhesitating conviction of a language-window, or hinge, through which it was possible to enter the London of the 1880s – and then, more disturbingly, as you accepted the author's invitation and gave yourself up to that world, the realization that the order of words, the names chosen, was prophetic. (*SS* xvii)

Prophetic of what is clear when Sinclair – both in life and dramatized in the novel – 'blacked out words' in the text 'until I achieved a sort of planchette message' (*SS* xvii). The message transcribed from this activity (it is reproduced in facsimile in the novel) reads:

> I took my Doctor and Netley through the course prescribed for surgeons ... struck the shoulder ... shattered the bone and grazed the subclavian artery ... fallen into the hands of the murderous ... removed to the base hospital. (*SS* xvii; *WCST* 59)

Could this describe the training, the murders and the supposed detention of Gull in an insane asylum? The 'Netley' in the text is a military hospital, but it also becomes the name of the queen's coachman. (One reason that the edition shown to Leper-Klamm is so valuable is the misspelling 'Nettley'; it was therefore a false prophecy and deserved its fate.) Sinclair claims that his method of deletion was drawn from the joyful linguistic refunctioning and visual design of Tom Phillips's *A Humument: A Treated Victorian Novel* (1980), but 'Sinclair' attempts a second treatment of the text, which, in his decision that it is 'better to take the flash of single words, cut phrases', more closely replicates the techniques of William Burroughs (*WCST* 60).

> *Netley. Surgeon. Horse ...*
> *Let us have some fresh blood, he said.*
> *Transparent fluid. Dull mahogany colour.*
> *A brownish dust.*
> *The stains are a few hours old.* (*WCST* 60)

This reads like one of the murder scenes as described by an imagist poet. 'Dictation at this speed,' comments 'Sinclair', 'takes the scribe ... so fast and so deep that he writes it before it happens', as Conan Doyle supposedly had, by producing his prophecy a year *before* the Ripper murders, 'and by writing it he causes it to happen' (*WCST* 61). But if Conan Doyle had encoded the murders once, Sinclair has done it several times in several ways.

In Sinclair's third narrative strand, which features the Victorian materials, Knight's 'castlist', the three Ripper suspects and several others, is vividly brought to life in tightly written omniscient narrative, with none of the debunking humour or irony found elsewhere. As Sinclair's Acknowledgements declare: 'The Victorian characters lived under the names that I have given them: their behaviour is dictated by sources other than historical record' (*WCST* 211). Such record shows Sir William Gull was a pioneer of many medical techniques, including the development of a patient-centred approach to healing, based on the belief that a doctor is treating not a disease but a person. One of his appreciative patients was the Prince of Wales, whom he successfully treated for typhus, and this contributed greatly to his social standing. He died a rich man in 1890; irregularities over his death certificate immediately spawned the fiction that he had lived on, incarcerated in an insane asylum.

The first three chapters from the Victorian strand slowly unfold the story of the orphaned Gull's education at the hands of a parson, in a world dominated by the Protestant work ethic. The conduct motto, 'Whatsoever thy hand findeth to do do it with thy might', ironically hangs over the future Ripper (*WCST* 28). This fervour, combined with the peculiar intensity of the child, produces a messianic interior life he shares with no one. 'We are the first ones, the chosen. This is our Ark. The world is water'

(*WCST* 28). The funeral of his father – he is borne upon the water that had carried the fatal cholera that killed him – is witnessed by Gull, 'his red eyes brilliant in a blackened face, his cropped hair ashed into age, an old man' (*WCST* 46). While Gull is usually presented as an unnervingly self-possessed and rationally wilful man, he 'screamed over the reeds in savage laughter' in a demonstration of his hidden (and future) self (*WCST* 46).

James Hinton, whose 'theology edges ... into sadism', as Sinclair puts it, was a doctor who believed that pain was a perfect replacement of the Christian sacraments (*WCST* 164). 'Why should I disturb the pain that is the only truth?' he asks in his final letter, in 1875 (*WCST* 178). It is through such fictional letters – those most gothic props of authenticity and narrative distanciation – that Sinclair cleverly focuses on moments of Hinton's career, leading up to his meeting with Gull. His life, his masochistic wallowing in pain, his fantasy of sexual intercourse with his wife's sister, are framed in terms of self-martyrdom. Eighteen thirty-eight finds the young man taking a night walk through Whitechapel, punctuated by 'shrieks in the night', which introduces Hinton to the pains of the flesh and to the institution of prostitution (*WCST* 83). His revulsion sows the seeds for his part in the Whitechapel murders, and the prostitutes' invitation to him, 'Come up and be dead!' seals the fate of their co-workers half a century later (*WCST* 84). Prostitution is a sacrifice of women, which can only be redeemed and cleansed by further sacrificial murder. Lost on 'this silken rim of hell' (*WCST* 83), Hinton cries out prophetically, 'Christ was the Saviour of men, but I am the Saviour of women' (*WCST* 84). By 1861 he is lodging with Gull, and is the eminent fleshly doctor's ascetic shadow, the one coolly observant through his 'dull mollusc eyes', the other raving and quoting apocalyptic verses concerning the Whore of Babylon from the book of Revelation (*WCST* 126). 'Prostitution', Hinton exclaims, 'is dead. I have slain it' (*WCST* 127). Gull corrects him: 'The sacrifice will only be complete with the willing consent of the victim' (*WCST* 127). Hinton ignores Gull's prediction of complicity (to which I will return in my discussion of *Downriver*); he says, 'Know that I am appointed time's abortionist' (*WCST* 127).

Sinclair's characters are clearly no longer Stephen Knight's simple accomplices to murder and conspiracy, but embodiments of single-minded obsession and evil, not unlike the Sons of Albion in *Suicide Bridge*. Chapter 18 shows Hinton attempting to become 'time's abortionist' by carrying out a proto-Ripper murder some years before the event, possibly on one of the eventual victims. He navigates between St Anne's Limehouse (a Hawksmoor church) and St Mary Matfellon, landmarks that 'Sinclair' and Joblard pass in their parallel narratives. Indeed they disturb time by intuiting the failure of Hinton's attempt: 'Hinton cops out ... Whips it, fans the fire, then refuses to follow his reasoning to the death' (*WCST* 151). In heightened detail, the narrative shows Hinton's attack on a prostitute. He 'touches the tip of her womb' during intercourse, but 'he cannot finish it', although he 'throws a coin at her feet', prefiguring the Ripper's actions (*WCST* 141). 'Hinton is terrible: Mosaic wrath' (*WCST* 142), Sinclair writes, but 'his prophecy is barren' (*WCST* 143). Hinton's mania 'causes' the conflagration of St Mary Matfellon. Perfectly preserved bodies of children are discovered in the ruins.

The fire which destroyed St Mary Matfellon occurred in 1880, five years after the historical Hinton's death. It is Gull who is 'time's abortionist' after all, since it is he who has created this asynchronous narrative. Later in the book, confined to the asylum under an assumed name, Gull dreams 'the outline of Mary Matfellon. His dream was the nightmare that Hinton had lived. He absorbed Hinton's death into his own' (*WCST* 205). But his own death is also a fiction, following his terrifying 'commission in lunacy' (*WCST* 191), at which he declares, 'I have been mad a long time, in a dream of men, of duties' (*WCST* 191), one of which is the dream of Hinton's 'duties', which he assumes as his own. He had witnessed his father's funeral; he lives to witness his own: 'He is free of his own history', a fiction (*WCST* 302). In his 'posthumous' anonymity, he trains the 'coachman' and the 'painter' to enact his will. He rebuffs the attempt of psychic Lees and Inspector Abberline (both lifted from Knight's account) to interview Lady Gull about Gull's whereabouts on the night of one of the murders, by appearing in unlikely drag as his own wife: 'Flattened nipples painted around with star-shapes, mapped skin: Sir William Withey Gull' (*WCST* 173). But through the successive stages of his insanity he experiences dissolution of this identity and ego, until 'Gull felt in his belly a stirring, a movement, something that he could not name, unknown, too slight to name; unstoppable. A child' (*WCST* 206). Unsexed, sealed in madness, Gull has – too late – fulfilled Hinton's false prophecy: 'The child that is born shall be an Antichrist, god of unreason, Babylon' (*WCST* 142). But even that prophecy is a fiction, located in Gull's dream of Hinton's failed act of murder.

The murders of 1888 escape direct depiction (and therefore re-enactment) in *White Chappell, Scarlet Tracings*. The disappointment of some readers at this forces them to confront their own prurience, the sin of which Sinclair is accused by Oliver in the letter quoted in *White Chappell, Scarlet Tracings* (which I described in the previous chapter). Sinclair has encountered evil again, but at the end of the novel he promises to bring his children to the site of Gull's childhood home. 'And the connection will be made, the circuit completed,' he concludes, a little too easily (*WCST* 210). Awareness of the innocence of children is prompted by his reading of Oliver's letter; 'They have no shadow of the future to chill their milky eyes,' 'Sinclair' realizes (*WCST* 166). This epiphanic release, however, is not the last word on the issue, because the shadow of the past is too strong to be annulled.

If Sinclair consistently presented his interleaving chapters as discrete, safely leaving the spectre of speculation in its historical chapters, or as exemplary 'windows' on the 1880s, his novel would read like Ackroyd's *Hawksmoor*, as a conservative confirmation of historical parallels and the unchangeability of the human condition. In chapter 29, however, he allows the 1970s and the 1880s to interpenetrate, and raises a new 'castlist' of London suspects. Robert Louis Stevenson's allegory of transformation, *Strange Case of Dr Jekyll and Mr Hyde* (1886), is presented as an analogue of the real life London medical case of Joseph Merrick, the 'Elephant Man', so called because of his disfigurement, and of Dr Frederick Treves of the London Hospital in Whitechapel, who had rescued him the year Stevenson published his novel (and two years before the Ripper murders). In terse paragraphs, Sinclair narrates how Treves nurtures his 'natural man', as a kind of Hyde, 'to absorb him, to give fire to his own nature, to the hidden being within', much as Gull had used Hinton (*WCST* 153). (The historical Treves did indeed call Merrick, a 'primitive creature'.)[13] Between paragraphs treating this story, 'Sinclair' meets Joblard in the pub, at first again misidentifying Joblard as that other orphan, Gull, who indeed transpires to be the subject of their lurid speculations. 'Unless we can *exactly* repeat the past, we will never make it repent,' says Joblard, as they prepare to engage the pub's stripper for a private show, in which she will wear the (elephant) head of Ganesh (*WCST* 150). But Sinclair, who comments that 'all writing is rewriting', knows the contamination of the past with the present will never be a truthful facsimile (*WCST* 149). It will never be repeated or repented by something in a mask. It may only be mis-repeated, as it were. 'Sinclair', with the help of cannabis, transforms into Shiva; like Hinton (or Sinclair's idea of Gull's Hinton), he becomes a false god. The chapter ends with an eerie scenario of Treves and Merrick looking at a girl on a bed. An old woman, who could be a midwife, is killed, it appears, by Treves's coachman. (The historical Treves believed that the presence of women would humanize Merrick, a view cruelly parodied here.) Treves hoists Merrick 'above the body of the girl, so that he stares directly into her face' (*WCST* 155). The word 'body' suggests she is dead, and the desire for Treves to see through the 'natural' eyes of his medical freak suggests a need for a vicarious *sensationalism* at this ambiguous scene. In the Whitechapel doctor, Sinclair has nominated another Ripper suspect, suggested another set of shadowy motives.

It is no surprise to find that 'Sinclair' remarks, 'We want to assemble all the incomplete movements ... until the point is reached where the crime can commit itself' (*WCST* 61). If so, then the resultant assemblage – a cubist portrait rather than a detective fiction 'Sinclair' says – declares its artificer guilty, not least of all because false evidence produces the true crime, in a multiverse of enactments, a parallel series of infinite terror and pain, the unimaginable multiple cruelty of so many murders of the same victims. Indeed Sinclair later criticizes Ripperologists as 'those who keep the pain alive by describing its parameters', identifying 'the truly guilty men' as 'the writers', like himself.[14] Everybody is necessarily guilty, even the prurient reader. Each theorist produces 'an authentic replica' of his or her 'own making' (*WCST* 198). Lies thus access truth, as 'Sinclair' lectures Joblard at the end of the novel, adopting a defensive position of radical scepticism and renunciation. 'I can't believe in *anything* I say. I repudiate this disbelief. ... I am ... re-writing a past that never, in fact, occurred' (*WCST* 198). The advantage 'Sinclair' has over Stephen Knight and the other nostalgists of evil is that he knows this. Sinclair guiltily realizes the damage done to the integrity of the continuing present, by insane multiversal versions of the past, in believing that 'the Whitechapel deeds cauterized the millennial fears, cancelled the promise of revelation', which is to agree with Hinton that the murders were in some way 'necessary' (*WCST* 61).

DOWNRIVER

Downriver (1991) is subtitled *A Narrative in Twelve Tales*, a formulation which deliberately avoids the word 'novel', and which suggests that we should not call its divisions 'chapters'. However, the word 'tale' does not quite fit, although it does perhaps suggest the short horror narratives of Edgar Allen Poe, or even the nautical romances of Joseph Conrad (both of which are relevant to the thematics of *Downriver*). No 'tale' may be excerpted and read individually. Rather than constituting episodes, the 'tales' overlap and leak into one another. Narratives (usually the stories of particular characters) can last several pages, or dozens; elements of one story can surface in another tale, hundreds of pages hence. This strains the book's necessary linearity, although the later chapters are more self-contained. In other words, the book is an intratext in its own right and it alarmingly connects with narratives in other parts of Sinclair's work, and intertextually, with other works of art. Necessarily, only a limited number of its narrative strands will be examined in this chapter.

Angela Carter grasps at the apposite analogy of the river to describe the phenomenology of reading this work: '*Downriver* is jam-packed with teasing little hints at possible plots ... These stories, flowing all together, form a river without banks in which you sink or swim ... clutching at associations, quotations, references to other writers.'[15] It is, to revert to a familiar metaphor, an attempt to create a Moorcockian 'multiverse'. The hero in the book is London itself; despite a castlist to match a Dickens novel, no individual human consciousness claims its centre, although 'Sinclair' again appears as a narrator, reliable or otherwise, until he dismisses himself and appoints a proxy narrator towards its end. Several novelistic 'rules' are broken. There is no consistent point of view; omniscient voice mixes uneasily with the first-person 'Sinclair'. Narrative continuity is not much regarded, and time sequences shift. It is almost a relief to discover that only one character, Arthur Singleton, the cricketer/tramp, and possible Ripper candidate, appears to travel through time. Yet even a book it significantly resembles, James Joyce's *Ulysses* (1922), for all its stylistic heteroglossia, focuses on three central characters.

If the city is the hero, supporting characters are the river and the overground railways, the arterial routes which connect (and thereby constitute) the city. This is not a novel (or a city) of the motor vehicle. *Downriver* presents a city of pavements, platforms, tunnels and quaysides (Sinclair's obsession with roads will have to wait until *London Orbital*). Viewed in this way, the overlapping tales attempt to mirror the complexities of urban space as that is described by postmodern geographers such as Iain Chambers, who offers a condensed and evocative summary 'of cultural complexity, most sharply on display in the arabesque patterns of the modern metropolis', in a description which is already packed with literary and aesthetic analogies:

> Here the narrow arrow of linear progress is replaced by the open spiral of hybrid cultures, contaminations, and what Edward Said has recently referred to as 'atonal ensembles'. It is a reality that is multiformed, heterogeneous, diasporic. The city suggests a creative disorder, an instructive confusion, an interpolating space in which the imagination carries you in every direction, even towards the previously unthought.[16]

The city itself is a chaotic, discontinuous multiverse. Its spaces are often imaginary, and negotiating them will be an imaginative activity. Indeed, Sinclair himself calls the city 'a theatre of possibilities in which I can audition lives that never happened' (*LC* 7). While Joyce supposedly believed that the Dublin of 1904 could be recreated from his novel, Sinclair knows that his fractured (mis)representation of 1980s London throws such a conceit into question. The book is heterogeneous and its apparent confusions are designed for imaginative engagement, not for mental reconstruction. This almost novel, this collection of incontinent tales which, not unlike Italo Calvino's *Invisible Cities* (1972), consists of possible multiple descriptions of the *same* city, reveals a multiple space, like that of the 'modern metropolis' itself, that opens out onto further questions – the 'previously unthought' – rather than presenting straight answers. In this aspect of his book, Sinclair is classically postmodern; his writing raises questions of ontology, the status of the distinct worlds he creates in his multiverse. In Brian McHale's formulation, while modernist fiction raises questions of epistemology (what the reader can *know* about Dublin from *Ulysses*, for example),

> postmodernist fiction deploys strategies which engage and fore-ground questions like ... 'Which world is this? What is to be done in it? Which of my selves is to do it? ... What happens when different kinds of world are placed in confrontation, or when boundaries between worlds are violated?'[17]

All these questions are relevant to an overall reading of *Downriver*; which London, or whose London, we are reading at any point is crucial. It is not clear how a narrator could relate events from which he is absented, if they are not his 'fictions'.

Although Sinclair's writing plays with these concepts – and the term multiverse is a powerful one to allow these questions to remain unresolved – he sometimes has distinctively *pre*-modern formulations of textual power, as in the divinatory superstition that dominates *White Chappell, Scarlet Tracings*, and is evident in *Downriver*. Indeed it is in his first novel that *Downriver* has its origins, as Sinclair has explained: '*Downriver* ... started out as a series of tales that would give some kind of meaning to the pain of the victims of Jack the Ripper, whose voices had, I felt, been left out of *White Chappell*. There was no female sound in there.'[18]

Fortunately *Downriver* did not remain this intended intratex-ual footnote to *White Chappell, Scarlet Tracings*, but developed into Sinclair's major fictional project; however, there are traces of his original intentions in the section entitled 'The Prima Donna's Tale', which is contained in tale 7, 'Prima Donna (*The Cleansing of Angels*)'.

This short narrative reads like a missing chapter from *White Chappell, Scarlet Tracings*, and attempts, in the victim's apparent voice, to renegotiate Gull's unanswered contention that 'the sacrifice will only be complete with the willing consent of the victim' (WCST 127). Angela Carter declared that the classic gothic opening, 'I had not, I think, been dead beyond two or three months when I dreamed of the perfect murder' (DR 202), begins 'better than Lovecraft, almost as good as Poe'.[19] 'The limpid narrative achieves genuine supernatural horror', as the reader witnesses the testimony of the 'Prima Donna', the last known victim of the Ripper.[20] She is not granted her historical name, Marie Jeanette Kelly, posthumously post-identity; it is a perfect murder because she is already dead. Similarly, although a blind surgeon (and Gull is figured as blind at the end of *White Chappell, Scarlet Tracings*) is admitted by a servant to the Prima Donna's room to participate in a series of rituals, he is not named. Far from being limpid, the narrative is deliberately defamiliarizing. As a ghost, the narrator steps free of her own personality, as 'I' slips evasively into 'she'; she watches 'the girl's face ... her legs raised as if for the stirrups' (DR 203). But she is clearly in control of the rituals with the surgeon. 'I drained him, I milked his venom ... My tongue went into his mouth like a fish that becomes a knife ... to make him speechless as well as blind' (DR 206). These rituals of emascula-tion – he is unsexed like Gull – also involve assimilation. 'She pressed him from behind. She held him until her life was his life. Her pulse in his wrist. Now her hands acquired his skills' of both healing and wounding (DR 207). As Gull had absorbed Hinton, he 'absorbs her anger, and her strength. He will act for her and *condemn himself beyond all hope of remission*' (DR 208). She becomes, in effect, not merely a shift of pronoun, but her own nameless butcher and perfect murderer (joining the eminent company of exquisite suicides in *Downriver*): 'She holds, in her hands, the womb – in which she should have been conceived: she is reborn' (DR 209). This miraculous resurrection dissolves into the objectivity of a third person narration, which ends in the horrified heteroglossic cry of the Victorian age: 'A gay woman, an unfortunate – disembowelled. Throat cut to the spinal cord, kidney on thigh, flesh stripped from the ankles. *Horror!* Lock it, seal it, bury all trace' (DR 209).

The surgeon is returned to his madhouse, defeated by his acts. The unspeakable rite of *White Chappell, Scarlet Tracings* is enacted at last. In that book, such a narrative would be framed by humour, but in *Downriver* only further horror contextualizes this set piece. 'Sinclair', the author of *White Chappell, Scarlet Tracings*, receives an invitation to meet an obsessive misanthropic Ripperologist, John Millom, who has not only erected a monument over the grave of the Prima Donna, but is witnessed transporting its soil (in his pockets) to his flat, where he has assembled 'a necrophile altar' upon which to construct a 'mud bride' for his 'vermicular marriage' (*DR* 212). The discovered document is a standard gothic plot device, but the one Sinclair 'copies' here is claimed to have been dictated to Millom from 'the madonna of that oven of meat' herself. (*DR* 202). They each offer an interpretation of the text, 'Sinclair' with a deliberately feeble Platonist account of the 'madness of love-death', Millom with a more plausible account of the woman as avenging angel, working through the surgeon to destroy him, a cleansing of, and by, the angels (*DR* 210). The dawning realization of 'Sinclair' that he is himself the author of this piece – which was too horrible to publish – shifts responsibility for its contents from Millom to himself. But worse is to come when 'Sinclair' examines the gift Millom leaves him: it is a copy of his own *White Chappell, Scarlet Tracings*, annotated by Millom (who protests against the Ripper candidature of Gull in exclamatory marginalia), hollowed out and filled with the 'contraband earth' from the grave, into which is pressed the impression of the asylum key that Millom claims belonged to the killer (*DR* 214). Millom had promised to name the Ripper; in a manner of speaking, he does. When a (blind) worm, memorial of both the surgeon and his 'willing' victim, emerges from the mud hollow, it is clear (again) that the truly guilty men are the writers like Sinclair (and their readers, like Millom). If the necrophile has already been compared to a bibliophile – 'he collected dead whispers. He walled himself in bad faith, in fantasies of decay' – the equation can clearly be reversed (*DR* 212). This indirect ethics of responsibility is resurrected from *White Chappell, Scarlet Tracings*. The worm of this fiction is as deadly as the Christian serpent. Postmodern fictionality cannot will the bad faith away. Sinclair detects guilt at the heart of any work of fiction, since it embodies both prophecy and enactment.

No amount of authorial guilt can assuage the fact that the victim's 'voice' remains unrecorded in this disputed act of ventriloquism supposedly from beyond the grave, remote, disembodied, barely human. As Rachel Potter explains, picking up on Sinclair's prospectus for the novel: 'Women ... are heard in terms of a generic 'female sound' and not as individual voices.'[21] Indeed, while many of the male voices, 'Sinclair' and Joblard for instance, are clearly dominant, it is not quite true that 'Women's bodies are figured as bit roles in the novel; they are victims of serial rapists, the protagonist in politicians' masturbatory fantasies'.[22] The Prima Donna has demonstrably more power than that within her narrative; and the second 'protagonist' hinted at here, Edith Cadiz, is more than the reduced sum of her exposed sexual parts, as will be shown. However, Potter draws attention to an extraordinary essentialist paean to women's combined 'anger' and 'strength' in the voice of 'Sinclair' (DR 183), which echoes the exhortation of these 'female' qualities, the same 'maternal metaphor', in the Prima Donna passage, quoted above.[23] '"Real" gender', concludes Potter, is 'reduced fictionally to an enslaved and degraded category.'[24] While not denying that Sinclair's female characters are often his weakest (and that masculinist bonding is almost a hidden theme), Potter's adverb 'fictionally' alerts one to the complexities of representation, to the 'arabesque patterns' of postmodern reality and fiction. As Angela Carter notes, some characters 'are drawn, kicking and screaming ... from real life', but she explains that Edith Cadiz 'is no less haunting a character because Sinclair makes plain she is not his own invention but the invention of another of the characters he has also invented'.[25] Like the postmodern city, avenues of reality and the imagination meet at an undecidable crossroads, an arena of 'creative disorder'. Cadiz's 'ambiguous reality status' releases her from the most obvious power-relations, and enables her to re-inscribe these relations, destabilizing notions of identity, and therefore gender.[26] Like the Prima Donna, her victimhood is not so singly a matter of individual voice or of degraded category. Despite Sinclair's episodic essentialism, we should trust his tales rather than their tellers.

Cadiz's story is actually the narrative of her invention, the invented narratives that are ascribed to her fictional 'being', the account of her disappearance, and her posthumous existence as a ghost, like the Prima Donna, haunting the narrator and his narrative. The actor Roland Bowman first tells 'Sinclair' of an acquaintance, a Canadian performance artist, the unlikely named Edith Cadiz. (Elsewhere, Sinclair confesses that the name was lifted from a tombstone's 'obliterated inscription' (*DS* 288).) Bowman's story – possibly his invention, as Angela Carter hints – becomes confused in the narrator's mind with a framed antique erotic photograph in Bowman's kitchen. Bowman tells of a strip show that Cadiz supposedly performed, wearing an unlikely 'costume of maps' of historical London (*DR* 63). As the crowd – confused by her act, abashed by the same effrontery of her nakedness that had attracted 'Sinclair' to the photograph – calls out place-names, a trained dog 'pulls away a Spitalsfield terrace with a twist of its powerful neck' (*DR* 63). It is not London that is revealed – the book's hero – but her fictive nakedness. She is – one transatlantic immigrant drawn to London, and frequently quoting another, T. S. Eliot – the corporeal 'waste land' beneath the place. This account – the reader receives it third hand – is followed by an imaginary omniscient narration of the rest of her life story: as a nurse tending mentally disturbed children, and – partly since she cannot survive on a nurse's wages – as a prostitute. This establishes a punning link between the worlds of 'Horse Spittle' and 'Whore's spital' (*DR* 78). Her chief punter is a Labour politician, Meic Triscombe, who is capable of sexual arousal only at his own Bevinite rhetoric (and clearly is impotent politically as opposition to the Thatcherite ascendancy). She is forced to have sex with his dog, an event from which she escapes the effects by narrating to herself further stories (see the passage I examined earlier). One answer to the koan-like riddle with which *Downriver* both opens and closes, 'What is the opposite of a dog?' is clearly a man like Triscombe (*DR* 3, 407).

It is partly Cadiz's desperate script that Bowman enacts in the abandoned synagogue in Princelet Street, becoming both the MP's dog and Edith herself, as she is re-embodied: 'But Edith Cadiz was instructed by her angel and would suffer no governance. Roland, naked once more, had the body of a woman' (*DR* 117). She is already an angel herself. She is last glimpsed alive, attending the MP's consecration of the site of the Aboriginal cricket match of 1868. He, like 'Sinclair', admires the essential strength and anger of this woman, but concludes, 'He wanted her to be buried alive' (DR 87). As mysterious men move towards her at the end of the chapter it is implied that he is about to have his wish fulfilled.

Downriver is full of supernatural train journeys. (Millom's 'gift' is opened on a train and, in an extended passage, 'Sinclair' analyses Tenniel's railway illustration to Alice in Wonderland, like a demented Michel Foucault interpreting Velasquez's Las Meninas, to which the Tenniel is compared. Tenniel's image operates like Conan Doyle's fiction in White Chappell, Scarlet Tracings, a window on imperialist mythologies, to help identify those guilty of various railway murders.) The arterial railways were constitutive of one of the components of modernity: the fixed chronometrics of the timetable, which made time an 'exploitable resource' (DR 171). 'Sinclair', travelling the neglected North London Line, counters this image of modernity by winding a Victorian time-piece backwards. He thereby creates a version of the postmodern 'interpolating space' populated by 'atonal ensembles' of his own discordant imagination. Immediately a Canadian 'Voice' can be heard, mediumistically ventriloquizing the words of the writers Eliot, Stella Bowen and Mary Butts in an intertextual séance, about the pain of the city. Eventually the 'Voice' materializes as an entity, an authoritative victim, beyond identity and time, like the Prima Donna. 'I knew I was looking at Edith Cadiz, the invented (and self-inventing) victim. I had no idea how to release her, or how to procure my own escape ... I no longer have place in this, even as an unreliable witness,' admits 'Sinclair' (DR 175). The result of this stalling of time is that 'night and day' become 'a single moment', full of 'future terrors'; Cadiz embodies the 'damage and hurt' of London, which she both performed and out of which she was imagined (DR 175). As Cadiz 'escapes', un-inventing herself in Sinclair's imagination, she melts into images of the Blitz that had turned London into a nightmare more startling than that evoked by the hellish 'Waste Land' of Eliot, whom she quotes so often. The 'guilty river' is a 'quisling' for having exposed the hero-city to aerial attack (DR 175).

If one of the markers of urban postmodernity is the growth of heterogeneous diasporas and the development of a 'hybrid culture', one might expect Downriver to reflect London's multicultural reality, particularly in the light of Sinclair's passionate plea for an understanding of the motives and mechanisms of historical immigration. Contemplating Spitalfields' Heritage Centre's setting up of a 'Museum of Immigration', he comments:

> As if immigration could be anything other than an active response to untenable circumstances – a brave, mad, greedy charge at some vision of the future ... It can always be sentimentalized, but never re-created. It is as persistent and irreversible as the passage of glaciers and cannot ... be codified, and trapped in cases of nostalgia. (*DR* 136)

This proposed museum is largely concerned with memorializing Jewish immigration of a century before. Indeed, Peter Brooker is correct in arguing that, in *Downriver*,

> the newer ethnic community of Bangladeshis, whose great Mosque now occupies the site of a former synagogue in Whitechapel's Fournier Street, are as if invisible. Bengalis are twice observed in groups, once having sex in their break from work and once shifting leather goods up to the West End ... Sinclair throws out the accusation that 'Banglatown, as it was vulgarly known, replaced the perished dream of Spitalfields'.[27]

However, Brooker neglects to point out that this renaming is part of 'the occult logic of "market forces"' (to which we shall return) as the very heritage industry that dreamed up the possibility of a museum of immigration gives way to the rampant commercialism of Brick Lane (*DR* 265). But the larger question remains. When the building of a Whitechapel mosque merely works to obstruct the 'unashamed voyeurism of the incarcerated onanist' resident in the 'Imperial fantasy' of the Monster Doss House, the Moslem culture is not invisible, it is blocking the view (*DR* 123).

There are two responses to this. One is to appeal to a respectful pragmatism. Sinclair is largely an autobiographical writer who turns those he encounters into monstrous parodies, into versions of his own history. While it might seem lame to suggest that he did not know members of 'the majority population of that area', it is true that Sinclair does not try to ventriloquize unknown contemporary others, a speculative white imagining in blackface, as it were.[28] Indeed, in his response to the proposed museum he recognizes the dual dangers of patronizing sentimentality and of a careless documentation. The comic juxtaposition of the imperial edifice of the Doss House and the othered 'muezzin who wailed his exotic arts ... to hurl fire and brimstone on the sublimely indifferent heads of sinners', reminds us that this is not a situation of postmodern social hybridity at all (DR 123). Indeed, Downriver was written in, and refers to, the shadow of the fatwa (or death threat) issued against Salman Rushdie for having depicted a diabolic Islam in The Satanic Verses (1988), an event which hardly warmed the literary intelligentsia to militant Islam. (There was, at this time, a banner across Brick Lane calling for the book to be banned.)[29] If we wish to see how the worlds of East and West inhere in one character, we must turn to texts like Hanif Kureishi's The Buddha of Suburbia (1990), and follow its trickster-narrator as he navigates the multiplicity of selves he has to accommodate, while living on the fault-line between cultures.

Secondly, it is possible to read Sinclair's obsession with London's colonial and postcolonial history, and earlier immigrations, which even Brooker accedes are 'an acknowledged, sometimes considered presence' in Downriver, as analogues for any migrant experience, to disentangle straight racial representation from diasporic consciousness (while not denying the historical specificity of individual situations).[30] It is possible to read the various Irish characters, or even the comic Hausa bookseller Iddo Okoli, who joins a dubious scam selling obsolete 'white goods' to third-world countries, in this way. Indeed a pile of Okoli's final book stock is described as 'the beached detritus of the Imperial Dream', and 'Sinclair' notices there a volume by Joseph Conrad, whose colonial parable Heart of Darkness echoes throughout Downriver (DR 15). Conrad's novel opens 'downriver' of London (before shifting to upriver Congo). His narrator, Marlow, noting, as does Sinclair, that London was established as part of a (Roman) imperial adventure and is forever marked with the signs of the postcolonial experience, remarks, 'And this also has been one of the dark places of the earth.'[31] Abandoned in an Estuary pub, appropriately called The World's End, Joblard shuffles Victorian postcards, 'as neutral as a Tarot pack' (DR 29), to create 'Joblard's HEART OF DARKNESS. A Narrative in Twelve Postcards' (DR 25). Suggesting, but not, in fact, predicting, the structure of the entire novel, these blurred scenes of imperial life offer a do-it-yourself world that is still unknowable and inexplicable. 'Is this faked photograph a rehearsal for an atrocity that has yet to be enacted? Or is it a reconstruction of some repellent episode, already well on its way towards entering the history books?' (*DR* 27–8). Like Conrad's unreliable narration, the reality evoked is ambiguous – the attitude respectful and distant – though here suffused with Sinclair's typical acknow-ledgement of the prophetic potentialities of artistic assemblage. Later in the novel Sinclair and Joblard take to the river in a parody of Marlow drifting with his city gentlemen, as they visit the wrecks and Thatcherite prison hulks 'downriver', a journey which ends in an apocalyptic 'shipwreck'.

Indeed, it is on that expedition that 'Sinclair' evokes the earliest – and best known – of his poignant tragedies of 'immigration', little narratives that bring the grand narrative of imperialism into sharp focus. He imagines the Native American Princess Pocahontas brought ashore there in the seventeenth century by her English husband, after the betrayal of her people. She is envisaged watching a Jonsonian masque at which she reverses the poles of civilization in a postcolonial act of abrogation: 'She maintained an unsurprised dignity before these spectacles of savage transformation: she-monsters deliv-ered of dancing puppets, clouds that spoke in rhyme' (*DR* 361). But her end – she dies of tuberculosis against which she has no immunity – exposes the unquenchable longing of the exile: 'Let her preach a quiet ruin upon the dockyards' that delivered her; 'Soon the forest will march back to claim her' (*DR* 362). A century later, Prince Lee Boo, sent by the people of the Pacific island Coorooraa to study glass-making, is 'imported into Rotherhithe as exotic ballast … It only required his rapid demise to convert him into a theatrical 'smash': an operetta with dances and sentimental speeches', an eighteenth-century equivalent of the museum of immigration (*DR* 52–3). Lee Boo also died of London's novel diseases within six months of arrival. In 1868 'King Cole', an 'Australian Aboriginal', led a victorious team against the MCC playing the imperial game of cricket (which features throughout *Downriver*). They are full of fear of 'the city of the Dog Man, the destroyers' of their civilization (*DR* 81) and, within two weeks, the destroyer of 'King Cole' himself: 'He found the infection he needed in cow's milk' (*DR* 83). It is in memory of this death that Triscombe delivers his bombastic consecration speech on 'the slaughter of a whole people, sacred innocents', while secretly calculating that this public exploitation of postcolonial history accrues little political capital (*DR* 86). 'There is no ethnic percentage in Abos,' he concludes (*DR* 86). It is at this event that we have the (last) sighting of Edith Cadiz alive, who, as a Canadian facing death in London (possibly at Triscombe's bequest), is another fated immigrant.

These cautionary tales, each from a different century, scattered throughout *Downriver*, warn that 'immigration' – that 'brave, mad, greedy charge at some vision of the future' – is fraught with mortal danger, and prepare the reader for the twentieth-century tale which is the most memorable of the book (*DR* 136). Although David Rodinsky, its protagonist, is not strictly speaking an 'immigrant', he is symbolically central to the now dispersed Jewish diaspora that once settled in the East End; his home was the very Princelet Street synagogue that was being converted into the museum of immigration, and was also the site of Bowman's theatrical metamorphosis into Edith Cadiz. Rodinsky, although a historical figure, is an avatar of Cadiz, since they both disappear into the metropolis.

In an attempt to make a Spitalsfield film for television, 'Sinclair' stumbles upon the local myth of Rodinsky, who was the reclusive and apparently scholarly 'caretaker and resident poltergeist' of the small synagogue, until one 'day in the early 1960s when he achieved the Great Work, and became invisible', seemingly abandoning the property and leaving his fascinating possessions of scribbled diaries and Talmudic studies (*DR* 134). Sinclair satirizes both the locals, the Newcomers, for whom Rodinsky is a 'feature' to boost house prices in these years of property inflation (*DR* 135), and the media functionaries with whom he futilely negotiates; his assigned producer is terminally 'lunched out' (*DR* 144). The attitudes of these indifferent groups contrast with the eerie and chastening experience of 'Sinclair' actually climbing to Rodinsky's room at the top of the synagogue, which had only recently been opened. Mainly narrated in the fifth tale, 'The Solemn Mystery of the Disappearing Room', 'Sinclair' realizes that the room is a 'trap' (*DR* 137), 'sucking in the unwary' (*DR* 138). The awful possibility that, as hinted at in the Conan Doyle-like title, 'The man remains, *it is the room itself that vanishes*' (*DR* 137) means that the 'psychic tourists' who visit the room cruelly cause Rodinsky to be 'assembled like a golem, in the heat of their attention' (*DR* 138). The room is a 'conjuror's smokescreen', which operates to trap the visitors into materializing (or imagining) Rodinsky in their own image, but without being able to restrain the image, exactly like a golem, the manufactured but uncontrollable mud homunculus of the Prague Jewish ghetto (*DR* 139).

Sinclair recognizes – in distinction to the heritage consciousness – that the true 'heritage is despair and the heritage is the measure by which we fail in visiting this grim module' (*DR* 138). One central failure is experienced when 'Sinclair' inspects the gnomic and mystical diary Rodinsky kept. Out falls a press cutting, a ghoulish photograph with the inscription, '*And here is Yasha, in this Nazi-released picture after his capture*' (*DR* 139). 'Sinclair' realizes the limits of his quest for knowledge. 'Why had Rodinsky preserved this image from among the mounds of unscissored newspapers? I was glad I did not have to know' (*DR* 139). Sinclair touches upon the inescapable connective imperative with which Derrida challenges our historical sense: 'If there is today an ethical or political question and if there is somewhere a *One must* it must link up with a *one must make links with Auschwitz*.'[32] This is the heritage of despair of the Jewish diaspora that the Newcomers disturb as the Rodinsky story breaks cover in the broadsheets.

Just as 'Sinclair' is about to rhapsodize over Rodinsky's room for his media contact in the terms used above, he is 'trump[ed]' by events (*DR* 146). One event is the discovery of an early photograph of the re-opened room which proves that the arrangement 'Sinclair' experienced so powerfully was 'entirely staged' (*DR* 147) with its 'books and romantic clutter' (*DR* 146). Secondly, (real) reports in the press lead to the receipt of three (real) letters attempting to delineate the historical Rodinsky. That they contradict one another – was Rodinsky a genius linguist or a subnormal dabbler? – opens the mystery (for Sinclair's subsequent non-fiction, as I have outlined in the Introduction), but shuts down the media project in *Downriver*. These letters, from those who had known Rodinsky, agree that he 'did not disappear' (*DR* 147) and 'neither was he invisible'

(*DR* 146). The fact that he died of a stroke does not solve the mystery of the room and its contents, including the fifty-three cases of books found there, but they serve as a cautionary tale for Sinclair's enterprise of collapsing fact into fiction. Significantly, 'Sinclair' consoles himself with a beautiful epiphany focused upon the Thames:

> The river *is* time: breathless, cyclic, unstoppable. It offers immersion, blindness: a poultice of dark clay to seal our eyes for ever from the fear and agony of life. Events, and the voices of events, slurp and slap, whisper their liquid lies: false histories in mud and sediment: passions reduced to silt. (*DR* 304)

A number of contradictory impulses are brought together here, but are not resolved, are left as a 'creative disorder', an image of the city and its stories through which the river flows. History, repeating itself, becomes not clearer, but a blind escape. Events (and their echoing histories) come and go, but reduce everything to passionless homogeneity rather than postmodern heterogeneity. It is a failure in the face of its uncertainty. 'Sinclair' fails to access the core of the mystery of the disappearing man, to penetrate the evasive heritage that lies at the heart of any immigrant experience. Only the immigrant – so often silent – may speak authentically with a subaltern voice.

Although a response to the various 'voices' surrounding Rodinsky, this epiphany comes late in *Downriver* where the focus has already shifted to the more straightforwardly satirical. *Downriver* carries the subtitle *The Vessels of Wrath*. God's omnipotence is proved by his endurance of those he dubs vessels of wrath, and by bestowing ultimate benedictions upon the vessels of mercy, the deserving compassionate.[33] Blake, however, thought that wrath was no sin and one of his proverbs, to which Sinclair may also be alluding, runs, 'The tigers of wrath are wiser than the horses of instruction.'[34] Sinclair, like Blake, is of the devil's party and knows it. In a more mundane sense, by the end of the novel, he is a vessel of wrath himself, full of anger, venting his satirical spleen. Indeed, he twice summons the Vessels of Wrath as though they were avenging angels. The epigraph to *Downriver* quotes another of Edith Cadiz's favourite authors, Mary Butts, describing the rather different 'wraths of shrapnel screaming down the air' during the First World War.[35]

Butts dramatizes her powerlessness, as she works in the East End, trying to maintain the decencies of civic society in the face of 'a nation driven past reflection', a phrase which more than adequately expresses Sinclair's own feelings about the 1980s (see also his contemporaneous samizdat poetry examined in the Introduction).[36]

Even early in the novel, in the tale 'Riverside Opportunities', for example, Sinclair turned that banal estate agents' phrase into an ironical description of the suicide by drowning of Tenbrücke, as he absorbs the whole of London and its river into his sacrificial being. However, it is in the chapters 'Art of the State (The Silvertown Memorial)' and 'The Isle of Doges (Vat City plc)' (tales 8 and 9) that Sinclair's wrath is the keenest, when it is focused upon the Thatcher government, particularly where it deals with its chief economic fiefdom, the fifty-five miles of neglected 'riverside opportunities' annexed by the London Docklands Development Corporation. 'The government's answer', wrote Robert Hewison in a perspicacious contemporary account,

> to the problem of regeneration has been to make the development area an adventure playground for market forces. Normal planning regulations have been relaxed, and at the pivot of the scheme is the Enterprise Zone where there are no planning restrictions at all ... The sums of money involved are a reminder that the private enterprise regeneration of Docklands is being achieved at public expense. The LDDC received £397 million in government grants ... With the firm political support of the Prime Minister, market forces will continue to enjoy their financially privileged playground.[37]

The Prime Minister is, of course, Margaret Thatcher, whose fictional analogue in *Downriver* is the Widow, who decides that her fifth term in office should be bolstered by the building of a monument to her dead husband (whose death in any case may have been 'managed' as a public relations exercise). (The analogy with Queen Victoria in this decade of repressive 'Victorian Values' is apposite.) This wild hyperbole, again reminiscent of Burroughs's satire on the ideological extremism of political leaders, has led some commentators to suppose that *Downriver* is set in the future. But the urgency of the Widow's demand that 'A State Commission must be set up immediately ... No planning permission is required. Flatten Greenwich if you have to', presents a relentless logic that feels quite authentic to the era.

This tale and tale 9 – which features the sequestration of the Docklands Isle of Dogs by the Catholic Church for its secret Voodoo headquarters (again a rather Burroughs-like conspiracy conceit) – are linked through Sinclair's belief in 'the occult logic of "market forces"', about which he is more forthcoming in an interview (*DR* 265). 'Thatcher introduced occultism into British political life. Her take ... verges on the demonic,' he says, explaining: 'She wanted to physically remake, she wanted to destroy the power of London, the mob, all of those things, which finally through the Poll Tax riots brought her down' (very suddenly, it is worth noting, before Sinclair's book was published!) (*V* 135). *Downriver* is an 'anti-demonic' satire because it tries to counter the ways Thatcher attempted this destruction: 'She opened herself up to the darkest demons of world politics, and therefore writers were obliged to counter this by equally extraordinary projects' (*V* 135). As we shall see, this unique approach gives strength to Sinclair's *vision* while weakening his *analysis*, as he enacts *rituals* of annulment. Once the bombastic monument is approved, two anti-projects are devised, one generated within the political system, the second outside it. The first, presented by a 'Professor Catling' (Joblard's own Jekyll), is to co-opt the surplus budget for the official monument to a performance art re-enactment of Scott of the Antarctic's failed attempt to reach the Pole in an artificially frozen dock (a parody of the real work of the real Catling, who, like Joblard, would be interested in the hidden shamanistic possibilities). The second is the attempt by the snail artist Imar O'Hagan to enact a ceremony against the Silvertown Monument by appearing as the Wicker Man, carrying dangerous fire into the centre of the official celebrations. Its effect is immediate. 'The Consort's Folly, the stepped pyramid (its lions, and friezes, and elevators) was a black torch. Flames tore at the sky' (*DR* 260). 'Sinclair' watches from his part in the Scott re-enactment: 'We had all passed unconsciously through some warp, crossed the border, and were viewing gospels of the future ... unvoiced witnesses' (*DR* 260). The book is not set in the future; it is set against it.

Rachel Potter criticizes *Downriver*'s 'negativity', because it seeks 'to gain access to forms of exchange outside the terms of this cash-nexus'; capitalism is simply occult.[38] She singles out

O'Hagan's gesture (but misses the strategic act of entryism 'Catling' performs, with its superbly funny account of the management of state-sponsored art), which she correctly sees as a shamanistic exercise. Potter claims that Sinclair's rituals mirror the commodified non-democratic society he satirizes: 'The self-selected position of the artistic shamans and the stance of witness by which Sinclair observes are forms of power taken by the individual not given by the group.'[39] As I argue throughout, such 'positions' are connected to constitute a 'group', even a culture, in Sinclair's thinking, operating as images of possible 'alternatives', not as a single oppositional programme. Potter is clearly adopting a Marxist position, but it is difficult to see how a democratic image of oppositional power could be developed in a work of art, how the horses of instruction might play their reasoned part more powerfully than the Vessels of Wrath. It is perhaps chastening to realize how original Sinclair's satire is because its vision does not conform to a recognizable political position; his thought ambivalently points towards the 'previously unthought' of postmodern space. Indeed, Sinclair denies he is a materialist at all, let alone a dialectical materialist, as his remarks on demonic Thatcherism with its occult capitalism suggest. In an interview he confirms that his 'Welsh' side believes in the divinatory power of writing, while this is opposed (Jekyll to his Hyde) by 'the Scottish side of me, which is … rational and cynical'. (V 59) While this points to a tension which Potter supposes exhibits bad faith, it explains the frequent ambivalence *Downriver* displays towards its own mythologies (Sinclair almost agrees with Potter when he argues the Blakean point that to oppose something is necessarily to confirm its power). It is ultimately this rich otherness, rather than its analysis, that makes *Downriver* a major novel. Like postmodern urban experience, it is an 'atonal ensemble' rather than a harmonized symphony, against which we find our own beliefs 'read'.

The account of the infiltration by 'Sinclair' and friends of the Isle of 'Doges', where the relocated Vatican is first discovered listening to Stephen Hawking explaining the concept of space-time, and is finally seen investing the Anti-Christ (Iddo Okoli in a newfound Voodoo role) as Pope, combines the perspective of the anti-materialist with the cynical rationalist. The Vatican undertakes a conspiracy to control the whole of Creation, scientifically and spiritually. If the ritual transportation of 'Sinclair' from the terrifying scene by a parody of Hawking's science is less than convincing, it does help to frame the entire episode as fiction, and asserts the primacy of the imagination, which has given it its only reality, and which can forcefully take it away:

> *Strengthen my disbelief* ... We had to believe more strongly in some other reality, a place beyond this place. To feel the curvature of time, which is love: to resolve the bondage of gravity. To move out along that curve, to have the courage to make that jump. I willed a mental picture of the only other site on the gulag for which I felt any affection (muted, ambivalent): the slight elevation of Mudchute. (*DR* 295)

This ritual transports 'Sinclair' to an unexceptional place, Mudchute, on the Docklands Light Railway system, which stretches this 'gulag' of market forces. The horrors of the Docklands are imaginatively annulled in honour of an emotion not often expressed in Sinclair's cosmology: love, the love that moves not just the stars, but space-time as well.

One travelling companion of 'Sinclair' is not so lucky; in the final tale of *Downriver* 'Sinclair' receives the companion's tongue, ripped out at the roots, a warning from the powers on the Isle of Dogs. However, the realistic, domestic setting in which this occurs – it is delivered through the post – alerts the reader to the fact that the previous chapters had contained hyperbolic fictions, though ones not quite in the control of the narrator 'Sinclair'. Like Prospero, he decides to relinquish his conjurer's power, knows he must bring the twelve tales of his book to a close. He expresses this hope in a letter to Joblard, pleading with him to narrate the final tale as his proxy. This laying bare of Sinclair's devices, in the manner of Nabokov or Beckett, a 'dreary post-modernist fraud' as Joblard calls it (*DR* 380), is motivated by the desire of both Sinclair (as author) and 'Sinclair' (as narrator) to 'get out from under the burden of a narrative which includes my request to be released from the burden of a narrative' (*DR* 378). This desire is also a matter of responsibility: 'I've hooked my credibility on to a pantomime of horror. I've exploited the darkest of times for comic routines that only flatter and fatten the monster.' (*DR* 379) By the time Joblard agrees, of course, even the text of the letter 'Sinclair' sends is re-presented through Joblard's supposed narrative. It is his own tongue that is excised (and may be the contents of the second Jiffy bag to be delivered to Joblard at the end of the book, although it is more likely to be the manuscript of *Downriver* itself, as a gift, the 'grimoire' or magician's book of spells). 'Sinclair' is entirely dumb during their final journey. Technically, this makes the tale slightly turgid through its lack of dialogue. If Joblard is not quite Molly Bloom, soliloquizing the valetudinary tale, from an entirely different point of view (there are too many of Sinclair's own verbal tics in the voice, perhaps deliberately foregrounding the artifice within the artifice), he is granted a teasing semi-autonomy to explore his own 'origins' on the Isle of Sheppey as an adopted child (Sinclair uses the more emotive term orphan), but 'Sinclair' has his revenge. He makes Joblard watch him participating in a ritual cricket match played in deep estuarine mud. A useless parody of all the cricket matches of the book (such as King Cole's), this is nevertheless an appropriate ending, since the ritual itself seems to stop time, the bogged down game even slower than the detractors of cricket commonly claim: 'I am without desire, and outside time,' concludes Joblard despairingly (*DR* 407). This is an altogether more English climax to the extinction of time than that found in Burroughs's work, whose final trilogy ends with an apocalyptic failure to overcome death; the bored Joblard declares he will 'just sit here, and keep my eyes firmly closed' until a taxi arrives to rescue him from the static scene (*DR* 407). The narrator 'Sinclair', who will never appear in the novels of Iain Sinclair again, is left stuck in the mud while the reader (and Joblard) are released from the narrative, which has become muddied with its pantomime horrors (if we trust the tellers of these overlapping tales). When the 'grimoire' is delivered to Joblard 'on his return', its accompanying note asks, 'I HOPE IT'S NOT TOO LATE TO CONSTITUTE A HAPPY ENDING?' (407). If 'happy' is understood to mean appropriate, what has to 'happen', then that hope may be entertained, albeit slenderly.

LANDOR'S TOWER

Landor's Tower is the second of Sinclair's four projected 'white chapel' novels, the one assigned to the West, and its tripartite structure reflects that of the first. It even begins reassuringly with the antics of the book-dealing *demi-monde* attacking the famous bookshop town of Hay-on-Wye, which reveals its matching cast of comic eccentrics and megalomaniacs. However, the reassurance is limited, because the opening of this narrative strand is suffused with a new element amid the typically self-reflexive narrations: the omnipresence of mortality. Sinclair's new self-conscious narrator is Andrew Norton, a less than successful writer, rather than the silenced 'Sinclair' of *Downriver*, but as he reflects on the imminent death of bookseller Billy Silverfish, he realizes his inadequacy to his literary task: 'Silverfish was a dead man, cancer of the tongue, but I didn't know it. Not then. I couldn't do a Dickens and play for sympathy' (*LT* 9). Norton is failing to complete a novel – a surrogate *Landor's Tower* – that attempts to constellate accounts of utopian communities, the disgrace of Liberal politician Jeremy Thorpe, a series of mysterious deaths in the defence industry, the haunted service station at Aust, and even the appearance of the Beirut hostage Terry Waite. These may not offer the frisson or imaginative scope of the earlier Ripperature materials, or the images of demonic Thatcherite capitalism, but they are consonant with Sinclair's spreading psychogeographical concerns and cultural politics. Norton is 'creeping West-ward', to use the title of the first book of *Landor's Tower*, to investigate the Welsh borderlands (and the English West Country), after years of an obsession with London; but the chosen territory actually returns Sinclair to one of his earliest influences. One passage of Alfred Watkins's *The Old Straight Track* identifies the Welsh locale of the novel as central to his theory of the ley line:

> There is a favoured spot – Llanthony – in the heart of the Black Mountains where primitive tracks and notches can be studied … There is little else in sighting points to be seen from the Abbey (it is always so called and should not be confused with a structure built by Father Ignatius 4 miles away in a different parish). But go to the top of the beautiful meadow on the way to Sarpel (sic), the site of the house which Walter Savage Landor … began but left unfinished, and there is plenty to be seen …The ley passes through the chancel of the original priory [40]

Landor's was not exactly a utopian community at Llanthony Abbey, more a one-man republic for the patrician retiree, but Sinclair's book focuses upon other failed attempts to locate or found communities in the same area: Father Ignatius' heretical monastery in the later nineteenth century, 'a spiritual gulag' (*LT* 180); Eric Gill's artistic harem (with poet-painter David Jones as its most morose member) in the 1920s, 'a prison colony, a pastoral hell' (*LT* 215); and the (fictional) poet Gwaine Tunstall's more recent attempt to found a post-hippie commune. The communities all fail, oppressed by religious or sexual mania and by acts of forgery, fakery and hypocrisy. The commune of hippies ends in a deserted farmhouse, with a leaky roof, its single paranoid occupant waiting for the latest police drugs bust.

The subtitle of Sinclair's novel is *Imaginary Conversations*, the title of one of Landor's better-known works, 'a great idea, but unreadable' as the novel itself says (*LT* 27). Landor, the 'perverse matchmaker' pitched real historical characters against one another in debate (Boccaccio and Petrach, for example) (*LT* 27). For Norton, as for Sinclair, such 'imaginary conversations', with their dialogic suggestion of community, provide the very definition of fiction. As Hitchings remarks:

> This kind of imaginary colloquy is a central motif of Sinclair's writing, in which the past and the present fuse together. Here, the fusion melds two distinct narratives: a contemporary one that smacks of noir-ish thriller and a historical one concerned with the endless search for utopia.[41]

Landor's Tower contains concentrated historical set pieces, for example, of Landor himself attempting to construct his tower, or of Brother Jonah spilling the diabolic beans on the famous incident when Father Ignatius supposedly brings a girl back to life in a necrophile ritual.

> I will never, however many years I am fated to live, forget the pathetic sight: the healing ravishment, the heretical and obscene acts Ignatius performed with the splintered wood which had soaked up the bright blood of Our Saviour. He made the corse his bride. And I was damned for witnessing this and keeping the truth hidden away for so many years. (*LT* 183)

One cannot get more gothic than the motif of the discovered manuscript of uncertain provenance, which has fallen into

Norton's hands. However, where similar historical materials in *White Chappell, Scarlet Tracings* have equal weighting with contemporary narratives, here they are fragmentary, epiphanic, abandoned, deliberately artificial. The illusion is visible and pleasurable; the prestigator's white gloves are always on show, whether they conjure Landor's buffoonery, or Henry Vaughan's intimations of mortality. Narratively framed as materials for Norton's abandoned novel, these materials are stolen by Norton's psychiatrist, offered for sale at auction and burned in a fire. The surreal picaresque of Norton's adventures leads to this literary immolation, in a hyperbolic pastiche, an excessive implosion of thriller plot devices, at the end of part 2, 'Siarpal'. *Landor's Tower* is a monument to abandonment, both Landor's and Norton's.

One of the subplots involves Rinkagate, a carnivalesque British political scandal involving class differences, a bungled murder plot, pet love and covert homosexuality: the affair between Jeremy Thorpe and Norman Scott, and Thorpe's apparent attempt to have Scott silenced. Trapped into a meeting with a hit man, Scott turned up with his massive Great Dane, Rinka. When the hit man shot his beloved dog, Scott caressed it, instead of running, and somehow the hit man failed to kill him. The historical hit man's name – never mentioned in the novel – was Andrew Newton, a near synonym to Andrew Norton. It is not surprising that, in the picaresque adventure towards the end of part 2, he is forced to re-enact, and thus re-narrate, the Scott incident: 'first time as tragedy, second time as farce' (*LT* 291). He rescues the Great Dane – 'The Dog Who Knew Too Much' is part of a Top Secret genetics experiment, and must be destroyed – and speeds off in a van, ignoring cheeky asides from the talking dog! (*LT* 276–7). Driving off a cliff, he is also re-enacting a scene from the (fictional) Jamie Lelage film *Amber Lights*. He is frozen framed in this moment, a culmination of a series of adventures that are the compounded intertextual borrowings of film scenes. As Norton disturbingly realizes, he is experiencing a state Sinclair elsewhere speaks of as a 'kind of temporal Esperanto, where nothing is real and everything is pastiched', the postmodern condition exactly, though animated to a nightmarish pitch (*RR* 149). He plunges to his suspended death, after swerving to avoid the apparently spectral reappearance of a character called Prudence Pelham.

75

Prudence is the equivalent of *Downriver*'s Edith Cadiz. She is acknowledged as Norton's 'Beatrice', despite the fact he is driven to kill her, if she has not already been killed by Kaporal, Norton's deranged researcher, in his own re-enactment of *Amber Lights* (*LT* 234). Norton is arrested and incarcerated in a mental hospital – although he mistakes it for a hotel – the narrative occasion for the insane hyper-reality at the end of 'Siarpal'. Norton first views Prudence in a Hay-on-Wye bookshop: the aestheticized epiphany he experiences is haunting and specific, and he significantly imagines its recurrence at the moment of his death.

> If my blood was to make one final charge on the brain, I'd freeze a single frame: Prudence in the bookshop, the blue flicker of a paraffin lamp. Face in shadow ... The first sight of her gave me access, so I hoped, to her past, her childhood, her lovers; access to experiences that were still to come. I wanted, from that one instant, to take possession of the woman, forcing her to invent the fiction of a life. (*LT* 67)

The fiction of her life might not be for her to invent, since Norton's relationship with her is already an 'imaginary conversation'. Prudence arouses suspicions (in Norton and in the reader) as she chatters about her lover 'Dai', which was the nickname of David Jones (*LT* 56). Far from being Norton's muse alone, she is at one point identified as being 'very – *very* – like the Jones muse, Prudence Pelham', who, a historical character, was one of the hapless Jones's love-obsessions (*LT* 255). Pelham married twice, and when she died in 1952, she left Jones a legacy. Norton's Prudence is lifted, as though from a portrait by Jones himself; this is suggested by the *fixity* of her pose in his epiphany, though the desire is carnal and essential: 'I wanted it. As most men do, many times a day, part of the baggage, the human contract' (*LT* 57). Yet when Norton is arrested, she metamorphoses into a military spy, yet another mystery of the 'defence industry'. 'Prudence was a false memory, a fantasy from another life,' Norton comments (*LT* 67). He apparently wants to kill her because of the flippancy with which she refers to the suffering Jones, his terrifying lifelong shell-shock, his depressed abandonment of literary fragments, such as his masterly poem *The Anathemata* (1952), confirming Jones as the major tragic artist-figure of *Landor's Tower*. 'I wanted to grip her by the shoulders, shake her, keep shaking her until she let the fantasy go. Until she accepted my version of what she was, how she should tell her story' (*LT* 69). She escapes, refusing Norton's attempts to narrativize her; like Norton himself, she belongs partly to another life, other stories. As her image fades, he realizes: 'I couldn't write what I could see' (*LT* 69). In his own writings, she 'was revealed as a literary device; a figure that symbolized virtue in an anaemic masque' (*LT* 289). 'I must kill the woman who provided the motivation, the only drive in my narrative,' says Norton at the end of book 2 (*LT* 292). It is clear, from another narrative strand, operating at a more literal level (the world of the marauding book dealers), that she may be an escapee from the asylum where Norton is placed, insanely obsessed with Jones. Indeed, since Norton's escape from thence is effected by a fantasy Prudence, who assumes a phantom corporeality, like Edith Cadiz before her, 'trapped within the spiral of a posthumous fable', she could just as well be his fantasy (*LT* 256).

Iain Sinclair, 'writing as' Andrew Norton, at one point in the novel, reads a crime novel by Ruth Rendell 'writing as' Barbara Vine. Norton recognizes immediately that the (unnamed) novel he is reading is the antitype of the fiction he himself is abandoning (partly in the face of Vine's brilliance). Norton still bears allegiance to the assimilative 'Great Work' of modernism, while his elaborate fictionality is playing with (and up) the ontological insecurities of postmodern narrative, never more so than in the plagiarized 'character' of Prudence (*LT* 31). Vine's novel offers carefully laid plants and payoffs, connections that are contrived, coincidences that are scribal tricks, plotted in advance, slotted in, professional and unimpeachable in their own terms. 'I relished the parallel worlds to which I had been granted access, but I was unnerved by the way she did it' (*LT* 30). At first sight this is a rerun of the debate between modernism and realism, but, for Sinclair, finally, the problem with Rendell/ Vine's work is the necessarily consensual nature of the mystery genre, or of any text that depends upon closure, or what Norton calls 'procedural tedium' (*LT* 36). He abandons Vine's book two thirds of the way through, before the questions raised are narrowed towards solutions, resolution. It offers a parallel world within a closed work, rather than an open work, as Umberto Eco defines it, one which does not fully engage a reader's participation.[42] Clearly there is little interest in such a procedure for a writer like Norton; he realizes that his work has another quality, as much an impediment as a liberation, an occult power or a lack of control: 'The creatures in my books have lives of their own' (*LT* 31). Norton questions what would happen if he demanded of Vine's characters what he demands of his own. 'What if I were to meet one of Vine's fabulous beings, out in the territory, in a location that I know?' (*LT* 31). He experiments with the mental unease this induces, by imagining he recognizes characters from real life in Vine's text, as uncanny as Prudence's transfigurations. Writing for Sinclair is a dangerous vocation, vatic, rather than consummated professionalism, its power predictive, its effects constitutive. The earlier use by 'Sinclair'of Conan Doyle's *A Study in Scarlet* is matched by Norton's use of Machen's *The Great God Pan* as another textual planchette (both are discussed earlier), but it is disturbing to see such an effect created by a contemporary realist text, that the magic potentially lies at the heart of any act of narration.

Modernist connectivity, as Norton confesses, is adhered to in *Landor's Tower*, and this is relevant to Sinclair's analogical use of Watkins's theory of the ley line as a theory of cultural formation, as outlined in the introduction to this book. Watkins's 'original revelation', Sinclair writes, is that 'everything connects and, in making those connections, streams of energy are activated. You learn to see. You forget to forget, to inhabit conditioned reflexes' (*LT* 12). This is, I believe, a very precise formulation, one that emphasizes the construction of the connections and the defamiliarizing, liberating, effect of what one then sees. It argues for intrinsic power not in the objects, but in the means of relation. Modernist juxtaposition, such as the ideogrammic method of Pound's *Cantos*, suggests that elements without syntactic linkage, by simple contiguous arrangement (or by drawing a line between them), create new combinations. Hugh Kenner wrote of the *Cantos*: 'The poem including history will contain not only elements and recurrences but a perceiving and uniting mind that can hope one day for a transfiguring vision of order it only glimpses now.'[43] Once we move from the technical, to the thematic, level, in both Pound and Sinclair, we approach ways of synthesizing a culture, or the creation of one that is not yet established. Pound made reference to 'what Frobenius meant by a *paideuma* – a people's whole congeries of patterned energies, from their 'ideas' down to the things they know in their bones'.[44]

One way in which Sinclair's cultural field is articulated is through personal association and friendship, rather than cultural mappings. Sinclair (like Pound or Yeats or even Kerouac and Burroughs) can be criticized for constructing a 'paideuma' from his friends, but, whatever its drawbacks, it is consistent with his distrust of the established cultural agendas. In *Landor's Tower*, an easily recognizable TV personality who wishes to explore Wales, snubs Tunstall, the communal utopian, who has fastidiously prepared a statement on the tragic David Jones, 'too sincere, too concentrated, – too slow for television' (*LT* 242). Sinclair often satirizes the brash wastefulness and indifference of the official British media when its limited agendas are confronted by a more extensive range of culture, popular or high. Tunstall himself is described as 'one of the best writers of [his] time, dismissed for being unknown, because the world at large was too lazy to search [him] out' (*LT* 116). The desire for Norton to introduce Tunstall to Joblard is founded on the fact he had published them both in his small press (as Sinclair indeed had published both Chris Torrance and Brian Catling, the pair's real-life analogues).[45] The meeting, in fact, barely takes place. The cynical Joblard 'wouldn't buy the notion of community ... "Hippie bollocks"' (*LT* 322). When they trek out to the farmhouse to meet Tunstall they find 'the utopian community shrivelled' (*LT* 334). Other than the narrator hearing the two poets' counterpointed snoring in the night, there is no (reported) interaction between them. This is a poignant as well as comic 'imaginary conversation'. It is Norton who hears the counterpoint, not the two sleepers. The lines of force lie in the relative connection (made by Norton here and by Sinclair in the act of writing), not in the two entities. Utopian community (or even the meeting of two artists) will always fail, but the utopianism, however ironically, survives in the connections established between them, located in a mind that is not the involuting vortex of a Pound, but the 'perceiving and uniting' (if paranoid) intelligence of Norton.

There are well over thirty other poets (let alone writers) referred to in this novel, and this fact may serve as an exemplary plotting of the cultural ley lines: from W. S. Graham to Charles Olson, from Dafydd ap Gwilym to Allen Fisher, from Ginsberg to Coleridge. These lines of connection suggest a virtual anthology more eclectic than Sinclair's *Conductors of Chaos* (or his semi-fictional 'Norton' anthology published as *Land/Or*). *Landor's Tower* ends with the series of 'Files recovered from Kaporal's Caravan & Research Notes (Presumed to have been written by Norton)' which provide information on Dorn, Gill, Father Ignatius, David Jones, Kilvert (who makes a brief appearance), Landor, Machen, Thorpe, the Vaughan twins – Thomas (the alchemist) and Henry (the poet) – Alfred Watkins, Vernon Watkins, West Country Suicides, and the two fictional analogues, Dryfeld and Lalage, most of whom are writers (*LT* 347). The reader may appreciate this as background, but it is neither a Poundian paideuma, nor a rogues' gallery, but something in between, more accurately, what Sinclair calls elsewhere a 'bibliography of ... associations' (*C* 121). Writers, as ever, are, however ironically, figured as central nodes of cultural energy, a 'perpetual symposium' of seers (*LOT* 155). These unlikely gatherings hint at the more explicit attempts to construct cultural mappings in Sinclair's non-fiction.

One of Norton's characters accuses him of writing novels with a predictable structure, so that, after the loose picaresque of a second part, the reader finds: 'Three: *quelle surprise*. A walk in the wilderness. What a cop-out, man!' (*LT* 285). But Norton defends himself when he notes of his tripartite structures: 'It was superstition: two men walking down a road will conjure the presence of a phantom third, the secret auditor ... The mysteries become transparent and the faces of the dead are lit with numinous radiance' (*LT* 288). This third book, called rather portentously 'Resurrection and Immortality' – the title of a magnificent trilogy of poems by Henry Vaughan – is certainly feeling towards that transparency, is unlike any other writing by Sinclair, and is certainly no 'cop-out'. The book does offer us such a walk (it is Norton and Joblard trying to reach Tunstall, superimposed upon memories of an earlier walk with Norton's schoolfriend). If so much of the novel is dedicated to bringing the dead to life (from Landor to Prudence, imaginary conversations shading into aesthetic necrophilia) – 'In the solid darkness beyond the window the dead gathered' – the robes of the necromancer have been exchanged for mourning, for an extended meditation upon death (*LT* 153). As Moorcock observes of *Landor's Tower*, 'It's tempting to describe the book … as a sort of picaresque Malory, but it doesn't march towards tragedy; rather it offers sardonic elegy.'[46] Unlike the unread last third of Barbara Vine's novel, abandoned free to the bookshop where Norton picked up Prudence, there are no resolutions, only resonances, or multiversal and intertextual openness.

Nevertheless, the novel does have (literally) a last word. The 'white chapel' to which Joblard and Norton trek, to find *their* phantom third, is St Issui at Patricio, as much of a pilgrim landmark, Norton notes, as St Mary Matfellon, the church burned down in *White Chappell, Scarlet Tracings* by the heat of Hinton's proto-Ripper sexual attacks. The memento mori upon its wall is a fairly literal but unsettling image of mortality for Norton. The other is the arrival of a small child, the third. Norton wants to photograph her but knows this method of recording – any method of documentary recording – would leave 'my camera raised like Death's hourglass' on 'the white-washed wall' of the chapel (*LT* 345). Called by her impatient mother, the girl is named 'Prudence', an image of mortality herself: 'I saw the face of the woman in the child' (*LT* 345). Her muttered words (the last of the novel), 'Mr Black. You're Mr Black', identify Norton with the deathly figure who follows Norton's Prudence through her life; already a memento mori, Prudence tells him, 'He only wore one shoe. The other foot was bare … with bones like a hand' (*LT* 239). She (mis)identifies former hostage Terry Waite as 'Mr Black' at one point, but the child Prudence is more prescient; the guilty, as ever in Sinclair's view, are the writers.

Behind many of these last pages lies Norton's (and Sinclair's own) memories of childhood, recollections of the Welsh New Year Mari Llwyd ritual, epiphanic flashes of early sexual encounters, and finally, painful memories of relatives losing *their* memories through the inexorable process of ageing. The great fear now is another aspect of the 'human contract'. Death, in *Landor's Tower*, is no longer a young poet's Heideggerian dream of a fully conscious culmination of being, figured as a variety of suicide, as it had been in *Suicide Bridge*. Neither is it something to be consciously overcome, as in Burroughs's influential mythology. Death is now a feared dissolution, an ever less conscious flaking apart of the self, a frightening loss of control and meaning. Pitched against the hopeful title of part 3, there is the reality of this dissolution:

> If memory went, I went: I knew all too well how my mother and my grandfather ... let it go ... The blood pudding of the brain was reduced to a rind, a desiccated cap ... There was only the shimmering past, events made fabulous by repetition: over and over, with no means of progression or resolution. (*LT* 318)

If 'resolution', in Barbara Vine's writerly procedures, is specifically rejected by Sinclair, then 'fabulous' is also a word he uses of Vine's creations, negatively. In the final analysis, there can only be those moments of 'lyric seizure' to energize the world (*LT* 31). The rest – the novel, poetry, the criticism of culture, the living of life itself – is the tracing of lines between those moments. The moments are real enough (even invented like all imaginary conversations); they provide our validating fictions, without resolution, but resisting dissolution.

3

Ambulatory Documentary: from Stalker to Fugueur

Sinclair's novel *Downriver* concludes with his note expressing 'gratitude to those twelve (unknowing) souls who accompanied me through my grimoire of rivers and railways' (*DR* 408). The ambulatory structure of the research for the tales becomes more evident towards the end of the book, since it is explicitly referred to, but is nevertheless not a narrative structuring device. However, the walking with friends, no longer anonymous and less 'unknowing', becomes the general structure of his documentary non-fiction from the 1990s onwards, particularly in the two contrasting works discussed here, *Lights Out for the Territory* (1997) and *London Orbital* (2002), although it is central to several other works of the period (and can be traced back to the more youthful running of the oracle in *Lud Heat*). Indeed, the tenth tale of *Downriver*, 'The Guilty River', could have found its way into a non-fiction context with little amendment. In its use of ambulatory investigation, and in its characteristic focus upon a forgotten or non-canonical writer and the places he or she inhabits (in this case the 1940s poet Nicholas Moore in Orpington and St Mary Cray), and in its acts of documentary recording (a long taped interview about Moore with the poet Peter Riley), this chapter is a model for Sinclair's subsequent non-fiction work. While many of the fellow walkers from the fiction are granted their historical names (so S. L. Joblard becomes Brian Catling once more), the vision is still uniquely Sinclair's. This egocentric vision saturates both books with passion and enthusiasm, but undermines their usefulness as historical record, even as Sinclair is offering – through recovering the (re)forgotten artist, the lost cultural artefact, and the unvisited locale with its buried history or invisible present – nodes of a constellated alternative culture. While these books have achieved a mainstream readership, the danger is that the audience responds more to the pleasures of Sinclair discovering outrageously interesting artist-figures for it than to his sincere and repeated invocations that it should investigate their works: by reading the poems of Moore, Riley and Catling, for example. While all three have been generously anthologized in Sinclair's *Conductors of Chaos*, in his non-fiction they risk being turned into celebrities, albeit anti-celebrities. The problem for Sinclair is that to evaluate and categorize in a literary critical way would necessarily involve him in negotiating the field of cultural and literary production as it is currently constituted, thus confirming the present positions and dispositions of the artistic world. For example, he would have to balance the cultural capital of the poetical avant-garde against the economic capital of the successful pulp writer, to assimilate terms from Bourdieu's sociology of art into Sinclair's polar obsessions. Instead of Bourdieu's neat but complex diagrams of culture, Sinclair prefers a literal map, a literal walk, and accidental collisions with culture (not just artistic culture, of course) along predetermined routes. Although Bourdieu's work is useful for showing how a new literary grouping 'makes its presence felt in the field of literary … production', how it 'modifies and displaces the universe of possible options', this model seems not to apply to the poetical avant-garde from which Sinclair emerged in the 1980s.[1] Neither does its insistence that displaced works become either 'outmoded' or 'classic', fit with the gestures of literary recovery Sinclair has undertaken on behalf of the 'reforgotten'.[2] While Sinclair's ambulatory approach avoids such cultural agendas, it denies the social and political determinations of artistic practice, and the cultural capital of permitted advocacy, in favour of empiricism (with a mystical edge; the collisions are often envisaged as predestined). If this work is, in Mark Rawlinson's words, 'as much a sorting through of the library created by London's street-level visionaries as it is a network of routes navigated by the author', the former relies upon the latter, cultural 'sorting' via literal 'navigation'.[3]

The modern urban wanderer, par excellence, is the *flâneur*, a figure that Baudelaire, for one, explicitly identified with the poet. Keith Tester summarizes: 'The *flâneur* is the individual sovereign of the order of things who, as the poet or the artist, is able to transform faces and things so that for him they have only that meaning which he attributes to them.'[4] He is both of the crowd, yet distant from it: the *flâneur*'s intense gaze – 'botanising on the asphalt', in Benjamin's memorable phrase[5] – is 'the gaze of the alienated man'.[6] This hero of modernity is at once entertained and rejected by Sinclair as his model of enquiry in *Lights Out for the Territory*, his '9 excursions in the secret history of London' (*LOT* iv). While agreeing at the outset that 'walking is the best way to explore and exploit the city', with 'drifting purposefully' as 'the recommended mode', later in the book an alternative term is introduced (*LOT* 4). 'We had moved into the era of the stalker; journeys made with intent walking with a thesis. With a prey' (*LOT* 75). Peter Barry's assertion that Sinclair has always inscribed 'his own mental biro-lines on the tarmac, and then excavat[ed] and link[ed] up the marked spots' both separates this ambulation from the 'botanising' dallying of the *flâneur* and reminds one of the essentially geographically conceived cultural theorizing of Sinclair, an activity that evokes a more modern term, which Sinclair has also flirted with, and even rejected on occasions: 'psychogeography'.[7] While the originators of this term, the Situationists, defined it as 'the study of specific effects of the geographical environment, consciously organized or not, on the emotions and behaviour of individuals', this should not be thought of as a scientific enquiry, but as more akin to the pranksterish interventions of Stewart Home's anarchist London Psychogeographical Association, which are treated sympathetically and hyperbolically in *Lights Out*.[8] Sinclair's mention of 'drift' as a mode of ambulation, evokes the famous Situationist *dérive*. Even the thesis that Sinclair states in *Lights Out*, that to stake out arbitrary routes for his walks on a map of London would 'vandalize dormant energies by an act of ambulant signmaking' (*LOT* 1), or *London Orbital*'s thesis that to circumnavigate the M25 counter-clockwise would undo the folly of the Millennium Dome, both suggest the modality of the *dérive*, which the Situationist International defined in 1958 as 'a mode of experimental behaviour linked to the conditions of urban society', or more specifically, 'a technique of transient passage through varied ambiences'.[9] These definitions are appropriate to Sinclair's work, with its insistently non-authorized views of London and its edge-land limits. However, in *London Orbital*, a further, much wilder term is introduced to describe the loosely circular journey around the orbital motorway. Sinclair and his fellow travellers are no longer stalkers; they are *fugueurs*. A fugue is a term for 'mad walking', a craze in nineteenth-century France that countered the *flâneur*'s reasoned ennui with escapes made by lunatics over incredible distances, 'a psychic commando course ... that makes the parallel life ... endurable' (*LO* 120). However, the contention that such 'journeys were a willed forgetting', the fugueurs unaware of their passage, seems unsustainable in the case of Sinclair's determined geographical excavations, his bricolage of found history (*LO* 120). 'The fugue is both drift *and* fracture,' he concludes, but it is still the stalker-magician who has staked out the route as an act of millennial annihilation, although the narrative of the walks is digressive and threatens to break down under the load of cultural references that Sinclair is positioning along the way (*LO* 120). Arguably, there are too many layers of memory. Whatever terms are best to describe the protagonists and their ambulations, Sinclair, in Brian Baker's echo of de Certeau's postmodern theorizing of urban space, 'is certainly on the side of the territory rather than the map, the fragmentary impressions of the walker rather than the totalized vision of the cartographer'.[10]

However, the two books differ in a number of important ways. *Lights Out* is an elaboration of essays written for various magazines, interspersed with accounts of walks constructed around routes drawn upon a map of inner London (and usually in the company of the photographer Marc Atkins). While the unforgettable opening shows Sinclair literally reading the graffiti of his environment as oracular utterances, the walks become less of a focus by the time the book ends with its ninth 'walk', which is principally an account of contrary traditions of British crime writing, the establishment figure of P. D. James contrasted with the elective outsider, Derek Raymond. The more accessible, but larger, *London Orbital* seems to have been conceived as a whole (although constellated by other non-fiction works) and dominated by its central conceit of walking the capital's 'grim necklace', to effect the Dome's annihilation (*LO*

1). Sinclair himself called the book 'the easiest I've ever done. The only one that's got a beginning and an end' (*V* 136). Turning Sinclair's recurrent metaphor of drift against him, Robert Bond comments on the effects of Sinclair's ease: 'Reading *London Orbital* is often more a matter of drift than of alert trust ... the text induces the conditions it diagnoses in orbital motorists: ... narcosis attendant upon perceptual overload.'[11] Bond regrets the autobiographical focus of the book, and suspects the sense of 'research being done, data accumulated, only in order to manufacture narrational idiosyncrasy and forced local history'.[12] While this is not entirely fair, the book's comprehensiveness does make it diffuse. For example, an uneventful and quotidian trip to a supermarket café, with its 'oasis of quiet conversation, unemphatic service, managed light', is hardly worth the retelling (*LO* 262). Even among the hymns of praise for the earlier *Lights Out*, there are dissident voices who sense a loss of critical edge in Sinclair's turn to non-fiction: 'The urgency of the writing has slackened. Sinclair has become a columnist, a garrulous personality explaining his London "walks",' states Ben Watson (who, by contrast, praises the political acuity of *Downriver* and the critically ill-favoured *Radon Daughters*).[13] Even readers who find clarity in Sinclair's explaining, and empathy in his personalizing, might agree with Watson's finger-wagging at Sinclair's 'interminable descriptions of failed films made by his circle', although even this 'secret history' works against simple charges of compromise and complicity.[14]

The best essays in *Lights Out* deliberately *dérive* from one topic to another within a few pages, keeping the reader's interest, and shaping the juxtaposed cultural elements; for example, in a very few pages of the first 'walk', the reader encounters Kurdish revolutionaries, Haitian exiles, maverick book dealers; witnesses Peter Fuller inventing a conservative artistic culture; samples the works of Richard Makin and Peter Riley; as well as visiting the sites of the decapitation of Jack the Hat, the former small press headquarters of Tom Raworth, and the bolthole of the Angry Brigade terror group (complete with recidivist poet), all down one road, a stone's throw from Sinclair's front door. On a grander scale, an arranged visit to the exclusive art gallery penthouse of Lord Archer – the book's *bête noir* – is juxtaposed with an account of the riverine botanical collection that Elias

Ashmole tricked out the Tradescant family in the seventeenth century. The unofficial history of Antonioni's London film *Blow Up* contrasts with descriptions of the austerity of Patrick Keiller's underground classic, *London*. Sinclair's ironical account of the collective amnesia of Ron Kray's public East End funeral can be read against the moving description of crime novelist Derek Raymond's Soho bar-room wake – both feed off London mythologies of the 1950s and 1960s – (but, in the first case, acts as a revisionary footnote to the excesses of Sinclair's own *Suicide Bridge*).

These concentrated attractions of urban life contrast with the more diffuse and muted surprises of London's uncertain margin in *London Orbital*. Acknowledging that the strange can also be banal, admits the fugueur's mad extended excursions into the book's method. Thus, Sinclair and his various walkers serially encounter, within the acoustic footprints of the M25, amid the *terra incognita* of the suburbs and edge-lands: retirement belts, paradise gardens, uninhabitable mushroom estates, road rage scenarios, snarling dogs, police in shades, many decommissioned asylums, 'asylum' seekers, as well as pristine steel and smoked-glass buildings that seem to have dropped out of the skies, like H. G. Wells's Martians, who also receive their dues for their fictional attempt to land at Woking. By contrast, Bram Stoker's Dracula picked the Essex estuary as bridgehead for his invasion plans, and is recognized as a fellow stalker: 'Dracula is the original psychogeographer, map fetishist, timetable freak' (*LO* 404). There are even mild encounters with 'paradigms of English eccentricity ... kindly ghosts deputed to hang about cafés, settling travellers on the right road' (*LO* 293). Reading the book is a leisurely rush, a dizzying stroll, as the 'grim necklace' becomes weighted with the rich overload of these narrative jewels. The resulting postmodern little narratives evoke a series of 'micro-climates', to use a term Sinclair borrows from the physical sciences, a series of (de)limited environments with their own conditions. The M25 is figured as a heart, as circulating blood, an image that counterpoints anatomist William Harvey to author Bram Stoker. The systems of control (whether vanished Thatcherite or ascendant New Labour) can only be seen and enumerated. But to see the centre from the periphery, to encircle it with so many stories – the voices of the living and the dead – and to criss-cross them with connections, correspondences and juxtapositions, is to move in upon the ideological centre, albeit imaginatively, with a vengeance. This could be a celebration of the postmodernist resistance of such little narratives to a grand narrative, but Sinclair sees that the powers of darkness are now all too human, and they are centred around the Millennium Dome, and its only begetters and its only worshippers, politicians of both major political parties. Sinclair's neat distinction between them suggests that his political edge is not as blunt as Bond and Watson suppose:

> Tories enact grand gestures that always result in land sales, asset stripping, collapse of public services. New Labour loves phantom government, virtual policies, obfuscation … The Thatcher method: the shameless lie, endlessly repeated, with furious intensity – as if passion meant truth. Blair lets it float, drift, until it's all too late; the shrug, the missionary smile, the shafting of another convenient scapegoat. (*LO* 291)

There are several characters in both books who operate rather like Peter Barry says David Rodinsky – who also haunts these volumes – does, as an 'avatar' of Sinclair himself.[15] To illustrate this, and a number of salient themes, as well as to bring them together as a conclusion (of both this chapter and this study), I will isolate, and concentrate upon, Sinclair's treatment of one such exemplary figure, in this case the visionary poet Aidan Andrew Dun, author of the epic *Vale Royal*. Of course, this is complicated by Sinclair's characteristic practice of linking such foci to particular locations and of intertextually connecting them to other artists. The title of the relevant chapter, 'X Marks the Spot', in *Lights Out*, suggests the association between alphabetic writing and place, and the identifications of cartography, although Sinclair is, as Baker points out above, in contact with what Jonathan Raban called the 'soft' city of evanescent perception rather than the hard city of physical geography.[16] 'Maps are a futile compromise between information and knowledge,' writes Sinclair, like a postmodern geographer; 'They require a powerful dose of fiction to bring them to life' (*LOT* 142). In a revealing summary of his unique version of psychogeography, Sinclair notes, 'I'd long held the fancy that the skin of London could be divided up by poets and seers as much as by families of gangsters' (*LOT* 142), and after listing his chosen spirits, he identifies a vacancy: 'King's Cross was up for grabs and Aidan ... was elected' (*LOT* 143).

The reason for Sinclair's self-confessed 'prejudice' in favour of Dun's *Vale Royal* is Sinclair's own 'failure', in a text predating *Lud Heat*, 'Red Eye', to attempt to capture the 'sense of the light-locked subterranean matter' of King's Cross/St Pancras, which – centring on writers connected to the area, like the two Shelleys – prefigures *Vale Royal*'s materials[17] (*LOT* 143). A 'prejudice', of course, is not a reasoned judgement, but Sinclair finds much to admire in Dun's work: the Blakean prophetic touch, the mystical sources, its focus on writers, and the fact 'it expresses London in terms of Egypt' (*LOT* 147). This reads like a description of a latter-day *Lud Heat*. 'The psychogeography of London is affected by the special pleading of the poem,' Sinclair says, using the Situationist term again in a prophetic – psychic geographical – rather than a strategic, sense (*LOT* 148). Yet Sinclair's own special pleading for the poem has its limits. He admits that *Vale Royal* is 'unspectacularly traditional in form, regular three-line units of bardic verse', contrasting with the 'drift of English modernism as expressed in ... Allen Fisher's *Place*' (or his own *Lud Heat*) (*LOT* 148). Dun merely 'reports on the vision rather than suffers it' (*LOT* 150), unlike the surrealist David Gascoyne or Barry MacSweeney, who is 'more urgent and implicated' (*LOT* 151). It is, finally, the heroic and isolated personality of Dun that fascinates, and Sinclair – true to form – stalks the poet down to his St Pancras territory.

Dun's X, his spot, on the landscape, is figured by Sinclair as a 'window' onto other historical periods, as Sinclair had once imagined Conan Doyle's *A Study in Scarlet* to be. Dun similarly reads Rimbaud's *Illuminations* (1886) as proof that 'the things that happened here' – such as Rimbaud's and Verlaine's brief sojourn in London – 'are eternal. They're on a loop' (*LOT* 155). Shelley, Chatterton, Boadicea, even Stephen Hawking (not unknown figures in Sinclair's own work, of course) coexist to found an 'Invisible College', 'a perpetual symposium' of poets and seers (*LOT* 155). The corollary of this, that 'what was happening had happened before', means the present becomes less particularized in one's experience, and takes on the delineations of the archetypal; prostitutes are read as angels (*LOT* 146). Sinclair praises 'the heroic persistence of reading the world in this way', both in *Vale Royal*, and in his guided tour around this territory by the slightly otherworldly Dun (*LOT* 149). It is significant that Sinclair wants to give Dun a copy of MacSweeney's own account of Chatterton, 'Brother Wolf', to widen the 'bibliography of ... association' he is constructing (*C* 121); he, Dun, and Atkins, set off on a rambling fugue to Camden. The real streets of North London proffer sites that are redolent with personal histories; references to Dun's old squat, and to an unofficial anti-university that had fructified him in his youth, point to vanished days of the counter-culture that Sinclair himself had attempted to register in his earliest documentary work, *The Kodak Mantra Diaries*.

One of the miraculous survivals of those years was the Camden bookshop Compendium, to which the trio is bound. Sinclair does not find the relevant MacSweeney book on the shelves, but they do meet Stewart Home delivering copies of his London Psychogeographical Society newsletter. When Sinclair asks parenthetically, 'How many ley lines must intersect here?' he is identifying the shop as a central node of an alternative culture, in a characteristic but unusually frank way, that confirms this study's sense of the ley lining of culture under-lining all of Sinclair's cultural criticism (*LOT* 156). The mysticism of Dun and the materialist pranksterism of Home meet head-on in a rather emblematic way. Like Joblard's meeting with Tunstall in *Landor's Tower*, the exchange is unresolved, more a juxtaposition orchestrated by Sinclair himself than a meeting of autonomous, or even sympathetic, minds. Indeed, this essay (fourth out of the nine) of *Lights Out*, is pivotal for Sinclair, as he toys with the alphabetic inscriptions of the routes he has carved on the map:

> Each essay so far written for this book can be assigned one letter of the alphabet. Obviously, the first two pieces go together, the journey from Abney Park to Chingford Mount: **V**. The circling of the City: **O**. The history of *Vale Royal*, its poet and publisher: an **X** on the map: **VOX**. The unheard voice that is always present in the darkness. (*LOT* 159)

If the stalker's process of inscription upon the map (and the subsequent tracing of the route over the territory) seems to offer a materialist (because empirical) account of culture, this is undercut by the 'unheard voices' that Dun, and through him, Sinclair, raise from the locales; Sinclair allows parts of his fourth essay to be suffused by the sensibility of Dun, without explicitly concurring with its constructions. But when Sinclair is asked, in the book-length interview with Kevin Jackson, conducted in 2002-3, 'Are you a materialist or not?' Sinclair replies, 'Not. Not at all, no. Far from … I'm absolutely one of those mad Welsh preachers who believes that … deliver the speech and you'll change someone's life' (V 59). This breathy refusal, with its affirmation again of the divinatory power of utterance, irritates Marxist readers of his work, like Bond and Watson. However, as in reading Blake or Yeats, it is important to take the unpalatable with the palatable. As Jonathan Dollimore has written of Yeats: 'To understand the poetry is not to transcend its violence but to enter its seductive sublimations.'[18] It is through such strange perspectives that we can judge ourselves, and our values, as we engage with the powerful otherness of these texts. They are, to use one of Sinclair's own metaphors, windows rather than mirrors.

Nevertheless it is important to see the weaknesses and strengths of Sinclair's unique perspectives, particularly as they relate to the cultural project that is at its most explicit in the non-fiction, but are everywhere in Sinclair's vast intratextual project. The strengths lie in the way the cultural scene is charted first-hand, unofficially, without the pre-existent social valuations inherent in any field of cultural production. The weaknesses lie in the project's reliance upon such contingency and personal experience and upon the mystical and numinous, and in its eschewal of (overt) theoretical or sociological positions. In the specific case of Dun, Sinclair's 'prejudice' for the poetic work places, into a privileged category, a poem that is arguably repetitious, arcane, and original only in its eccentricity. (The counterpointing of Dun and MacSweeney and Fisher, of course, indicates that there is an *implicit* poetics behind Sinclair's positions on poetry, but it is seldom expressed theoretically.)[19] The celebration of Dun's work elevates its creator into celebrity. The ley lines intercept; X marks the spot. To read Sinclair sympathetically is to feel the attraction to such a magnetic node, but necessitates a critical resistance to its pull. In the novels (and, to a lesser extent, in the poetry) this critical distance is granted to the reader by its very fictiveness. However, in the ambulatory documentaries, the reader has to remember that, like maps, 'they require a powerful dose of fiction to bring them to life', but this is a dose that requires the antidote of critical resistance in reading them, to isolate, and refine, their power (*LOT* 142).

Notes

INTRODUCTION. LOGGING THE CONTOUR LINES OF CULTURE

1. Nicholas Lezard, 'Meandering round the M25', *Guardian Review*, 21 September 2002, 14.
2. Julia Kristeva, *The Kristeva Reader*, ed. Toril Moi (Oxford: Blackwell, 1986), 37.
3. See Gilles Deleuze and Felix Guattari, *A Thousand Plateaus* (London: Athlone Press, 1988), 3–25.
4. Chris Torrance and Phil Maillard, 'Iain Sinclair/Lud Heat/Albion Village Press: A Tracking & an Interview, *Poetry Information*, 15 (Summer 1976), 7.
5. Andrew Hedgecock, 'Iain Sinclair – Renaissance Man of the Dying Days of the 20th Century', *The Edge*, 6 (1997), accessed at www.theedge.abelgratis.co.uk/sinclairiview.htm; page 2.
6. Iain Sinclair, 'The Necromancer's A to Z', *Guardian*, 14 October 2000, accessed at www.//books.guardian.co.uk/reviews/history; pages 1–4.
7. James Wood, 'Magus of the City', *Guardian*, 23 January 1997, 10:2.
8. See David Cooper (ed.), *The Dialectics of Liberation* (Harmondsworth: Penguin, 1968).
9. Peter Barry, *Contemporary British Poetry and the City* (Manchester and New York: Manchester University Press, 2000), 177–8.
10. Iain Sinclair, *LAND/OR: Poet's Poems No 9* (Belper: Aggie Weston's Editions, 2002).
11. William Cobbett, *Rural Rides*, vol. 1 (London: Dent, Everyman's Library, 1966), 74.
12. Barry, *Contemporary British Poetry and the City*, 177–8.
13. Ezra Pound, *ABC of Reading* (London: Faber, 1951), 22.
14. See Pierre Bourdieu, 'The Field of Cultural Production', *The Field of Cultural Production* (Cambridge and Oxford: Polity Press, 1993), 29–73. This work is returned to in chapter 3.

15. Iain Sinclair, 'On the Road, *Guardian Review*, 19 October 2002, 18–19.
16. Anon, 'Iain Sinclair's London Orbital, Barbican London', accessed at www.compulsiononline.com/lorbital.htm; page 1.
17. Wood, 'Magus of the City', 10:2.
18. Ibid., 10:2.
19. Henry Hitchings, 'Landor's Tower', *New Statesman*, 23 April 2001, accessed at www.newstatesman.co; page 1.
20. Simon Reynolds, 'Down and Out in London', *Village Voice,* 18–24 August 1999, accessed at www.villagevoice.com/issues/9933/reynolds; page 1.
21. Hitchings, 'Landor's Tower', page 1.
22. Lezard, 'Meandering', 14.

CHAPTER 1. POETRY: THE HARD STUFF. THE TOFFEE OF THE UNIVERSE

1. Rachel Potter, 'Culture Vulture: The Testimony of Iain Sinclair's *Downriver, Parataxis*, 5 (Winter 1993–4), 42.
2. Peter Barry, *Contemporary British Poetry and the City* (Manchester and New York: Manchester University Press, 2000), 173.
3. William Carlos Williams, 'Excerpts from a Critical Sketch: *A Draft of Thirty Cantos by Ezra Pound*' (1931), repr. in J. P. Sullivan (ed.), *Ezra Pound* (Harmondsworth: Penguin, 1970), 119.
4. Allen Fisher, 'A Confluence of Energies: A Reading of Iain Sinclair's *Lud Heat*', in Fisher, *Stane, Place Book III* (London: Aloes Books, 1977), 30/31.
5. Fisher, 'Confluence of Energies', 30/31.
6. Kerry Downes, *Hawksmoor* (London: Thames and Hudson, 1970), 206.
7. Barry, *Contemporary British Poetry and the City*, 178.
8. Ibid., 172.
9. David Harvey, 'From Space to Place and Back again: Reflection on the Condition of Postmodernity', in Jon Bird, Barry Curtis, Tim Putnam, George Robertson and Lisa Tickner (eds), *Mapping the Futures* (London and New York: Routledge, 1993), 11.
10. Harvey, 'From Space to Place and Back again', 21.
11. S. Foster Damon, *A Blake Dictionary* (Hanover NH and London: University Press of New England, 1998), 15.
12. William Blake, *The Complete Poems*, ed. W. H. Stevenson (London and New York: Longman/Norton, 1971), 625.
13. Ibid., 661.
14. Ibid., 780.

15. Donald Wesling, 'The Poetry of Edward Dorn', in R. W. Butterfield (ed.), *Modern American Poetry* (London and Totowa NJ: Vision and Barnes and Noble, 1984), 226.
16. Blake, *The Complete Poems*, 108.
17. Tony Lambrianou, *Inside the Firm* (London and Basingstoke: Pan Books, 1991, 12.
18. Blake, *The Complete Poems*, 661.
19. Ibid., 106.
20. Ibid., 105.
21. Lambrianou, *Inside the Firm*, 12.
22. Blaise Pascal, *Pensées* (Harmondsworth: Penguin, 1966), 215.

CHAPTER 2. MERE FICTION (I.E. IT HASN'T HAPPENED YET)

1. Roz Kaveney, 'Turn and Turn Again: Sinclair, Ackroyd and the London Novel', *New Statesman and Society*, 9 September 1994, 39.
2. Nicholas Lezard, 'White Chappell, Scarlet Tracings', 11 August 1995, accessed at http://proquest.umi.com/pqdweb; page 1.
3. Angela Carter, 'Iain Sinclair: *Downriver*', in her *Shaking A Leg: Collected Journalism and Writings* (London: Vintage, 1998), 197.
4. Peter Ackroyd, *Hawksmoor* (London: Penguin, 1993), 218.
5. Eric Mottram, *William Burroughs: The Algebra of Need* (London: Marion Boyars, 1977), 138.
6. Iain Sinclair, 'Unnaming the Nameless', in Camille Wolff (ed.), *Who Was Jack the Ripper?* (London: Grey House Books, 1995), 73.
7. Clive Bloom, *Cult Fiction: Popular Reading and Pulp Theory* (Basingstoke and London: Macmillan, 1996), 164.
8. Ibid., 164.
9. Ibid., 177.
10. Mottram, *William Burroughs*, 63.
11. Brian Catling, 'Spread Table, Spread Meat, Drink and Bread', an interview by Ian Hunt, *Parataxis*, 4 (Summer 1993), 56.
12. See Stephen Knight, *Jack the Ripper: The Final Solution* (London, Toronto, Sydney, New York: Granada, 1977), throughout.
13. Michael Howell and Peter Ford, *The True History of the Elephant Man* (Harmondsworth: Penguin, 1980), 199; pages 190–210. Appendix 3 carries Treves's own account of his dealings with Merrick.
14. Sinclair, 'Unnaming the Nameless', 74.
15. Angela Carter, 'Iain Sinclair', 199.
16. Iain Chambers, 'Cities without Maps', in Jon Bird, Barry Curtis, Tim Putnam, George Robertson and Lisa Tickner (eds), *Mapping the*

Futures (London and New York: Routledge, 1993), 189.
17. Brian McHale, *Postmodernist Fiction* (London and New York: Routledge, 1987), 10.
18. Sinclair, quoted in Rachel Potter, 'Culture Vulture: The Testimony of Iain Sinclair's *Downriver*', *Parataxis*, 5 (Winter 1993–4), 46.
19. Carter, 'Iain Sinclair', 201.
20. Ibid.
21. Potter, 'Culture Vulture', 46.
22. Ibid., 47.
23. Ibid.
24. Ibid.
25. Carter, 'Iain Sinclair', 198–9.
26. Ibid., 199.
27. Peter Brooker, *Modernity and Metropolis: Writing, Film and Urban Formations* (Basingstoke and New York: Palgrave, 2002), 103 (also quoting *Downriver*, 265).
28. Brooker, *Modernity and Metropolis*, 103.
29. Robert Hewison, *Future Tense: A New Art for the Nineties* (London: Methuen, 1990), 93.
30. Brooker, *Modernity and Metropolis*, 103.
31. Joseph Conrad, *Heart of Darkness* (London: Penguin, 1983), 29.
32. Jacques Derrida, quoted in Jean-François Lyotard, 'Discussions, or Phrasing "after Auschwitz"', in *The Lyotard Reader*, ed. Andrew Benjamin, (Oxford: Blackwell, 1989), 387.
33. Romans 9: 22–3.
34. William Blake, *The Complete Poems*, ed., W. H. Stevenson (London and New York: Longman/Norton, 1971), 110.
35. Mary Butts, *The Crystal Cabinet: My Childhood at Salterns* (Manchester: Carcanet, 1988), 94, also quoted in the fore-pages to *Downriver*.
36. Ibid., 94.
37. Hewison, *Future Tense*, 80–81.
38. Potter, 'Culture Vulture', 40.
39. Ibid., 46.
40. Alfred Watkins, *The Old Straight Track* (London: Abacus, 1974), 52–3.
41. Henry Hitchings, 'Landor's Tower', *New Statesman*, 23 April 2001, accessed at www.newstatesman.co.; page 1.
42. See particularly Umberto Eco, 'The Poetics of the Open Work', in Eco, *The Role of the Reader* (London: Hutchinson, 1981), 47–66.
43. Hugh Kenner, *The Pound Era* (London: Faber, 1975), 376.
44. Ibid., 507.
45. For example, Chris Torrance, *The Magic Door* (London: Albion Village Press, 1975); and Brian Catling, *Pleiades in Nine* (London: Albion Village Press, 1976).
46. Michael Moorcock, 'Saved by Mickey Spillane', *Spectator*, 7 April

2001, accessed at www.spectator.co.uk/...current&section=&issue=2001-04-07&id=358.

CHAPTER 3. AMBULATORY DOCUMENTARY: FROM STALKER TO FUGUEUR

1. Pierre Bourdieu, 'The Field of Cultural Production', *The Field of Cultural Production* (Cambridge and Oxford: Polity Press, 1993), 33. Fig. 2 on p. 49 is one such diagram.
2. Ibid.
3. Mark Rawlinson, 'Physical Graffiti: The Making of the Representation of Zones One and Two', in Susana Onega and John A. Stotesbury (eds), *London in Literature: Visionary Mappings of the Metropolis* (Heidelberg: Universitätsverlag C. Winter, 2002), 244.
4. Keith Tester, Introduction to Tester (ed.), *The Flâneur* (London and New York: Routledge, 1994), 6.
5. Walter Benjamin, *Charles Baudelaire: A Lyric Poet in the Era of High Capitalism* (London: New Left Books, 1973), 36.
6. Ibid., 170.
7. Peter Barry, *Contemporary British Poetry and the City* (Manchester and New York: Manchester University Press, 2000), 177–8.
8. *Preliminary Problems in Constructing a Situation*, from *Situationniste Internationale* 1, 1958, accessed at www.unpopular.demon.co.uk/lpa/ words, which is also the website of the London Psychogeographical Society.
9. Iwona Blazwick et al. (eds), *An Endless Adventure An Endless Passion An Endless Banquet: A Situationist Scrapbook* (London and New York: ICA/Verso, 1989), 22.
10. Brian Baker, 'Maps of the London Underground: Iain Sinclair and Michael Moorcock's Psychogeography of the City', *Literary London*, 2, accessed at homepages.gold.ac.uk/london-journal/march2003/ baker.html; page 3. Baker is referring to Michel de Certeau's chapter, 'Walking in the City', which may be found in Simon During (ed.), *The Cultural Studies Reader* (London and New York: Rouledge, 1993), 126–33.
11. Robert Bond, '*London Orbital*: a Walk Around the M25', accessed at www.literarydictionary.com/adverts/sinclairlondonorbital.html; page 1.
12. Ibid., page 2.
13. Ben Watson, 'Iain Sinclair: Revolutionary Novelist or Revolting Nihilist?', Militant Esthetix website, accessed at www.militantesthetix.co.uk/critlit/SINCLAIR.htm; page 8.

14. Watson, 'Iain Sinclair', 8.
15. Barry, *Contemporary British Poetry and the City*, 176.
16. See Jonathan Raban, *Soft City* (London: Flamingo, 1975), ch. 1, 'The Soft City', 8–16.
17. A relevant passage of 'Red Eye', appears in *Lights Out for the Territory*, 143–5; others in *Flesh Eggs & Scalp Metal*, 51–3.
18. Jonathan Dollimore, 'Art in Time of War: Towards a Contemporary Aesthetic', in John J. Joughin and Simon Malpas (eds), *The New Aestheticism* (Manchester and New York: Manchester University Press, 2003), 45.
19. Dun's work may be found in Aidan Dun, *Vale Royal* (Uppingham: Goldmark, 1995); MacSweeney's work may be found (with Thomas A. Clark and Chris Torrance) in the volume general-edited by Sinclair, *The Tempers of Hazard* (London: Paladin, 1993), 145–76. This was the volume Sinclair was hoping to find on the shelves of Compendium. Allen Fisher's work may be found (with Bill Griffiths and Brian Catling) in the same series, in *Future Exiles* (London: Paladin, 1992), 19–150, with an introduction by the present author, 11–17.

Select Bibliography

WORKS BY IAIN SINCLAIR

Note that some volumes have been republished subsequent to the original publication. The first significant publication or the first widely available publication is listed (or both, where that is important).

Fiction

White Chappell, Scarlet Tracings (Uppingham: Goldmark, 1987; republished: London, Glasgow: Paladin, 1988).
Downriver (or, The Vessels of Wrath) A Narrative in Twelve Tales (London: Paladin, 1991).
Radon Daughters (London: Jonathan Cape, 1994).
Landor's Tower (or, The Imaginary Conversations) (London: Granta, 2001).
Dining on Stones, or, The Middle Ground (London: Hamish Hamilton/ Penguin Books, 2004).

Graphic Novel/Short Stories

Slow Chocolate Autopsy (with Dave McKean) (London: Weidenfeld, 1997).

Poetry

Back Garden Poems (London: Albion Village Press, 1970).
Muscat's Würm (London: Albion Village Press, 1972).
The Birth Rug (London: Albion Village Press,1973).
Lud Heat (London: Albion Village Press, 1975).
Brown Clouds (Durham: Pig Press, 1977).
The Penances (London: Many Press, 1977).
Suicide Bridge (London: Albion Village Press, 1979).
Fluxions (London: Hoarse Commerz, 1983).

Flesh Eggs & Scalp Metal (London, Hoarse Commerz, 1983).
Autistic Poses (London, Hoarse Commerz, 1985).
Significant Wreckage (London, Words Press, 1988).
Flesh Eggs & Scalp Metal: Selected Poems 1970–1987 (London: Paladin, 1989).
Jack Elam's Other Eye (with Gavin Jones) (London, Hoarse Commerz, 1991).
Lud Heat/Suicide Bridge (London: Vintage, 1995).
Penguin Modern Poets 10 (with Douglas Oliver and Denise Riley) (London: Penguin, 1996).
The Ebbing of the Kraft (Cambridge: Equipage, 1997).
Saddling the Rabbit (Buckfastleigh: Etruscan, 2002).
Buried at Sea (Tonbridge: Worple Press, 2006).
The Firewall, Selected Poems 1979–2006 (Buckfastleigh: Etruscan, 2006).

Documentary

The Kodak Mantra Diaries (Allen Ginsberg in London) (London: Albion Village Press, 1971).
Groucho Positive/Groucho Negative (London: Village Press, 1973).
Lights Out for the Territory (London: Granta, 1997).
Rodinsky's Room (with Rachel Lichtenstein) (London: Granta, 1999).
Liquid City (with Marc Atkins) (London: Reaktion Books, 1999).
Dark Lanthorns: David Rodinsky as Psychogeographer (Uppingham: Goldmark, 1999).
Sorry Meniscus: Excursions to the Millennium Dome (London: Profile Books, 1999).
London Orbital (London: Granta, September 2002).
Edge of the Orison (London: Hamish Hamilton/Penguin Books, 2005).

Plays

An Explanation (with Christopher Bamford); produced in Dublin 1963.
Cards (with Christopher Bamford); produced in Dublin 1964.

Criticism

Crash (London: BFI Publications, 1999).

Other

White Goods (Uppingham: Goldmark, 2002).
The Verbals – Conversations with Iain Sinclair (with Kevin Jackson) (Tonbridge: Worple Press, 2003).

Edited or Introduced Volumes, Catalogues

The Shamanism of Intent: Some Flights of Redemption (Uppingham: Goldmark, 1991).
Conductors of Chaos (London: Picador, 1996).
Bill Griffiths, *A Book of Spilt Cities* (Buckfastleigh: Etruscan Books, 1999).
Alexander Baron, *Low Life* (London: Panther, 2001).
Arthur Conan Doyle, *A Study in Scarlet* (London: Penguin, 2001).
LAND/OR: Poet's Poems No. 9 (Belper: Aggie Weston's Editions, 2002).
London: City of Disappearances (London: Hamish Hamilton, 2006).

Recordings

Downriver (King Mob, 1998), recorded at The Instrument, London. Reading from the novel with interspersed audio atmospherics by Bruce Gilbert.
Prima Donna/River of Ghosts, Gaffer Hexam (with Iain Sinclair) (Foundry Records, n.d.). Very short passages from *Downriver* with songs inspired by the book.
Dead Letter Office: Poems 1970–2004 (Rock Drill 12, Optic Nerve for Birkbeck College, n.d.). A well-recorded, passionate reading of a wide range of work.

Film

Ah Sunflower! (Allen Ginsberg in London) (with Robert Klinkert), WDR TV (Cologne), 1967.
Diary Films (8 mm). Various, 1969–75.
Maggot Street (featuring B. Catling and Dermot Healey), 1972.
Three Sculptors (directed by Saskia Baron), BBC2, *The Late Show*, November 1991.
Photographing Whitechapel, BBC2, *The Late Show*, May 1992
The Cardinal and the Corpse (directed by Chris Petit), Illuminations Films, for Channel 4, 1992, *Without Walls*.
The Falconer (with Chris Petit), Illuminations Films made 1996–7.
Asylum (co-directed with Chris Petit), Illuminations Films.
London Orbital (with Chris Petit), Illuminations Films for Channel 4, October 2002. Available as video from Illuminations.

Uncollected Articles and Reviews

'Unnaming the Nameless', in Camille Wolff (ed.), *Who Was Jack the Ripper? A Collection of Present-Day Theories and Observations* (London: Grey House Books, 1995). The subtitle to the book says it all. The guilty ones, argues Sinclair, are the writers with their manifold answers to the question of the book's title.

'The Necromancer's A to Z', *Guardian* 14 October 2000. A review of Peter Ackroyd's compendious history *London: The Biography*. While full of praise for the detail of Ackroyd's book, Sinclair is critical of the conservative use of the past to ameliorate the poll tax riots and race riots of the present.

'On the Road', *Guardian Review*, 19 October 2002, 18–19. A puff for the Barbican event used to launch *London Orbital*.

'The Coat in Question', *London Review of Books*, 20 March 2003, 31–3. Masquerading as a review of David Seabrook's *All the Devils are Here*, this is a psychogeographical exploration of Kent.

'Diary', *London Review of Books*, 8 January 2004, 30–31. Largely an account of John Clare's life in Northampton.

BIOGRAPHICAL AND CRITICAL STUDIES

Books on Sinclair

Baker, Brian, *Iain Sinclair*, Contemporary British Novelists (Manchester: Manchester University Press, forthcoming). The volume will analyse Sinclair's texts with close intertextual reference to fiction by others who share a central concern with the imagination of London and with Sinclair's recurrent concerns. The monograph will consider: the insistence upon intertextuality and a language use which collides the demotic with the poetic; the implication of the author in the text, particularly the writing subject of the non-fiction, and the implied inter-relationship between life and text; the use of psychogeography as a way of rethinking urban space; the self-conscious use of myths of London, and particularly in Sinclair's archival interest in London writers and writings; the recurrence of the material text and material body within Sinclair's work; and the fragmented, fractured and obsessional subjects which feature in both Sinclair's fictions and non-fiction.

Bond, Robert, *Iain Sinclair* (Cambridge: Salt Publications, 2005). This study covers key texts and defines Sinclair with reference to London writing. The writing of the city is preoccupied with the relation between capitalism and religion. A cultural Marxist perspective is supplemented by the work of Bourdieu, which is used to examine why Sinclair is the sole representative of a neo-modernist poetical movement to achieve mainstream publication, and to examine Sinclair's elevation of the artist figure. Bond's originality lies in his thesis that in Sinclair's obsessive worldview, disinterested artistic compulsion is valorized over capitalism's self-interested productivity.

Articles and Other Writings on Sinclair

Anon., 'Iain Sinclair's London Orbital', an online version of the alternative culture magazine *Compulsion*, www.compulsiononline. com/lorbital.htm (accessed 1 April 2003). A useful description of the Barbican event used to launch *London Orbital*, suggesting the evening's variety.

Baker, Brian, 'Maps of the London Underground: Iain Sinclair and Michael Moorcock's Psychogeography of the City', *Literary London*, Issue 2, homepages.gold.ac.uk/lodon-journal/march2003/baker.html. Using literal and metaphorical notions of cartography, Baker compares Sinclair's *Lights Out for the Territory* to Michael Moorcock's epic *Mother London*. Sinclair reads London as a text; the pedestrian psychogeographer is heir to the flâneur of the nineteenth century, a troublingly ambiguous figure. On the other hand, Moorcock tries to bring into being a lost 'underground' London. But both writers resist traditional mappings that attempt to capture totality.

Baker, Kenneth, 'Dealing with Disappearing Characters', *San Francisco Chronicle*, 30 September 2001. An article that is actually an interview with Sinclair, in which he defends using minor political events, such as the Thorpe trial, in comparison with US writers using major ones.

Baker, Phil, and Mark Pilkington, 'City Brain: Iain Sinclair', an interview. A wide ranging interview, conducted following the publication of *Landor's Tower*. As its context implies, it focuses upon mysteries and disappearances, though it does allow Sinclair to talk about the process of plotting *Landor's Tower* over many years but of writing it very quickly. He expresses his scepticism about the term 'psychogeography', and vents his fears about the future of mainstream publishing. Foretean Times website: www.forteantimes. com/articles/147_iainsinclair (accessed 2 April 2004).

Barry, Peter, *Contemporary British Poetry and the City* (Manchester and New York: Manchester University Press, 2000). Focuses upon the early London-based poems. While he ignores many changes in Sinclair's work, he traces continuity from *Lud Heat* to a work like *Dark Lanthorns*.

Bond, Robert, '*London Orbital*: A Walk Around the M25', www.LitEncyc. com (accessed 27 March 2003). Short but perspicacious account of *London Orbital* that contrasts the objectivity of Ackroyd's *London* with what Bond sees as Sinclair's rambling and wilful book, whose political imperatives do not enable the reader to develop the critical distance found in earlier work.

——'Wide Boys Always Work: Iain Sinclair and the "London

Proletarian Novel'", *Literary London: Interdisciplinary Studies in the Representation,* homepages.gold.ac.uk/London-journal/bond.html (accessed 10 August 2003). An article that traces Sinclair's writing's relationship to the London proletarian novel, particularly with regard to resistance to the works ethic of dominant capitalist society. While the proletarian novelists Kersh, Kops and Baron were still tied to commercial publishing, Sinclair's neo-modernist writing has been freer to demand close study of its audience.

Brooker, Peter, *Modernity and Metropolis: Writing, Film and Urban Formations* (Basingstoke and New York: Palgrave, 2002). In chapter 4, 'Re-imagining London' (pp. 96–119), Brooker offers a succinct reading of *Downriver* and *Rodinsky's Room*, and criticizes Sinclair for his inadequate representations of women and of the multicultural vitality of the territory he claims to chronicle.

Carter, Angela, 'Iain Sinclair: *Downriver*', in Carter, *Shaking a Leg: Collected Journalism and Writings* (London: Vintage, 1998), 196–202. An early review of *Downriver* Carter praises the novel's apocalyptic scope. If she is the source for believing that *Downriver* is set in the future, she nevertheless sees the book as a phantasmogoric attack on Thatcherism.

Fisher, Allen, 'A Confluence of Energies: A Reading of Iain Sinclair's *Lud Heat*', *Poetry Information*, 15 (Summer 1976), 3–4. Reprinted, with minor changes, in Allen Fisher, *Stane, Place Book III* (London: Aloes Books, 1977), 30/31. One of the earliest accounts of Sinclair's work, from the fraternal point of view of a fellow British Poetry Revival poet at work on a similar project.

Hartung, Heike, 'Walking and Writing the City: Visions of London in the Works of Peter Ackroyd and Iain Sinclair', in Susana Onega and John A. Stotesbury (eds), *London in Literature: Visionary Mappings of the Metropolis* (Heidelberg: Universitätsverlag C. Winter, 2002), 141–63. Ackroyd and Sinclair are contrasted: the former is historical while the latter is geographical. While Ackroyd's narratives contrive to invent a trans-historical London, Sinclair is seen as playing off his fascination with the occult against his digressive involvement with other artists, leading to a restructured contemporary London.

Hedgecock, Andrew, 'Iain Sinclair – Renaissance Man of the Dying Days of the 20th Century', *The Edge*, 6 (1997). An interview in which Sinclair is revealing about his early fiction and his plans for *Landor's Tower* as a novel about failed utopian projects.

Hewison, Robert, *Future Tense* (London: Methuen, 1990). Contains a brief account of Sinclair's work, placing it in the context of other London writers. There is also an account of Rodinsky's room, written before *Downriver* was published, revealing Sinclair's first interest in the myth.

Hinton, Brian, 'Iain Sinclair', *Tears in the Fence*, 34 (Summer 2003), 115–17. A review of a number of books (by a character from both the fiction and the documentary) which acknowledges a valedictory tone in Sinclair's early-century works on London, recognizing its refocusing upon the suburbs for his future work.

Hitchings, Henry, 'Landor's Tower', *New Statesman*, 23 April 2001. Generally an enthusiastic review, particularly interesting on Sinclair's use of language.

Jarvis, Simon, 'The Cost of the Stumbling Block', *Parataxis*, 4 (Summer 1993), 36–41. Critical account of Sinclair's identification of certain poets as misplaced shamans, and a critical endorsement of the work of Brian Catling.

Kaveney, Roz, 'Turn and Turn Again: Sinclair, Ackroyd and the London Novel', *New Statesman and Society*, 9 September 1994, 39. Comparing the two writers, Kaveney acknowledges the complexities of Sinclair's plots, his ear for speech, but finds Ackroyd more polished.

Korn, Eric, 'Around the Landscape of a Dream', *Times Literary Supplement*, 5 April 1991, 26. A reluctant convert to Sinclair's nightmarish vision in *Downriver*.

Lezard, Nicholas, 'A Room Full of Emptiness', *Guardian*, 18 March 18. A sympathetic account of *Rodinsky's Room*.

—— 'Meandering round the M25', *Guardian Review*, 21 September 2002, 14. A perceptive review, acknowledging the intertextual aspects of Sinclair's *oeuvre*, and declaring *London Orbital* a 'hoot'.

—— 'White Chappell, Scarlet Tracings', *Guardian*, 11 August 1995. A short review, welcoming Sinclair's first novel back into print, but not neglecting to mention its connection to Ackroyd's work.

Livingstone, Ken, 'A City Seen Anew', *New Statesman*, 17 January 1997. While the author has no great literary insights, the former GLC leader and (then) future mayor of London praises Sinclair for his unofficial and detailed account of London, including areas that Livingstone 'represented' (politically) but discovered that he did not 'know'.

Moorcock, Michael, Introduction to *Lud Heat* and *Suicide Bridge* (London: Vintage, 1995). A disappointing introduction, in that it praises Sinclair for his fiction's focus upon the capital city and makes distinctions between him and others, such as Martin Amis.

—— 'London Pride', *New Statesman and New Society*, 8 March 1991, 36. An impressionistic review of *Downriver*, praising the Celtic visionary perspective of the author.

—— 'Saved by Mickey Spillane', *Spectator*, 7 April 2001. A sympathetic review of *Landor's Tower*, which he recommends to newcomers to Sinclair's *oeuvre*.

Penman, Ian, 'A Magus Marooned', *Guardian*, 5 May 2001. Laments Sinclair's *Landor's Tower* as a tired literary performance, devoid of the magic of earlier pieces.

Perril, Simon, 'A Cartography of Absence: the work of Iain Sinclair', *Comparative Criticism* 19 (1997), 309–39. An excellent account of Sinclair's 'compulsive associationism' and his cartographic imagination. Perril defends Sinclair's discovery of the invisible in the visible, the unknown in the known, from charges of transcendent shamanism, by showing how Sinclair's works present a self-conscious parallel universe.

Potter, Rachel, 'Culture Vulture: The Testimony of Iain Sinclair's *Downriver*', *Parataxis*, 5 (Winter 1993–4), 40–48. A critical account of Sinclair's novel, lamenting its lack of female characters, and the subservient role of women within the fiction; it also attacks Sinclair for lacking a coherent social and political vision.

Rawlinson, Mark, 'Physical Graffiti: The Making of the Representation of Zones One and Two', in Susana Onega and John A. Stotesbury (eds), *London in Literature: Visionary Mappings of the Metropolis* (Heidelberg: Universitätsverlag C. Winter, 2002), 233–53. A wide-ranging article, on Ackroyd and Moorcock as well as Sinclair, it analyses London writing as tending towards the non-generic in its opposition to consumer culture and counter-culture. While de Certeau's methodology is found too schematic for the contemporary breakdown of the distinction between 'hard' and 'soft' cities of earlier writings, Sinclair is seen as a crucial practitioner of such manipulation of the temporal and spatial networks of London.

Reynolds, Simon, 'Down and Out in London', *Village Voice*, 28 August 1999. Review of *Lights Out for the Territory* and *Liquid City*. Traces the influences of Keiller and the Situationists on Sinclair's documentary, but criticizes both the famous rush of verbless sentences and the effect of overdoses of erudition.

Samson, Ian, 'Books: Toffee of the Universe', *Guardian*, 23 January 1997. One of the few reviews of Sinclair's verse, which recognizes its 'brilliant, lapidary thoughts and well-honed observations'.

Sheppard, Robert, 'Artifice and the Everyday World: Poetry in the 1970s', in Bart Moore-Gilbert (ed.), *The Arts in the 1970s: Cultural closure?* (London: Routledge, 1994), 129–51. The section 'Naming the Rocks in a Larger than National Way: Prynne, Fisher, Sinclair' considers these poets as heirs to the geographical impulse of Charles Olson.

—— 'Iain Sinclair, Suicide Bridge', *Iron*, 29 (July–September, 1980), 23–4. One of the book's first reviews.

—— 'When Bad Times Made for Good Poetry: Iain Sinclair's *Autistic Poses*', in Ludmity Gruszewskiej Blaim and Malcolm David (eds),

Eseje o Wspótczesnej Poezji Brytyjskiej i Irlandzkiej (Gdańsk: Wydawnictwo Uniwersytetu Gdańskiego, 2005), 104–18. An account of Sinclair's period of greatest neglect, concentrating on a booklet issued in less than twenty copies in 1985.

—— *Where Treads of Death* (Liverpool: Ship of Fools, 2004). A pamphlet collecting four reviews produced as appendices to the present volume; also published as: 'Where Treads of Death', a review of *The Ebbing of the Kraft*, published on the Pores website, www.bbk.ac.uk/ Pores (2004); 'Guessed Disappearance', a review of *Rodinsky's Room*, *Stride*, 2002; 'Fugueurs in a Landscape', a review of *London Orbital*, *PNR*, 149 (January 2003), 86; and 'DRACULA plc', a review of *White Goods*, *Poetry Salzburg Review*, 5 (Autumn 2003), 43–8.

Torrance, Chris and Phil Maillard, 'Iain Sinclair/Lud Heat/Albion Village Press: A Tracking & an Interview', *Poetry Information*, 15 (Summer 1976), 7–12. Important early interview, plus some notes contextualizing *Lud Heat*.

Watson, Ben, 'Iain Sinclair: Revolutionary Novelist or Revolting Nihilist?', Militant Esthetix website: www.militantesthetix.co.uk/ critlit/SINCLAIR.htm. A provocative essay. While full of praise for *Downriver*'s political incisiveness with regard to its depiction of Thatcherite Britain, and while presenting one of the few positive readings of *Radon Daughters*, which he declares a masterpiece, Watson sees the non-fiction of the late 1990s onwards as an attempt to present a watered-down version of his previously uncompromising and uncompromised vision. The severest criticisms are reserved for Sinclair's anti-leftism, and his attacks on Trotskyites, which Watson suspects of coming dangerously close to fascist anti-progressivism.

Wolfreys, Julian, 'Undoing London or, Urban Haunts: The Fracturing of Representation in the 1990s', in Pamela K. Gilbert (ed.), *Imagined Londons* (New York: State University of New York Press, 2002), 193–217. A study of London artists, including Sinclair – *Lud Heat* is taken as exemplary of his *oeuvre* – whose representations of London eschew both the objective and subjective viewpoints in favour of a fragmentary sense of consciousness and place that escapes totality.

Wood, James, 'Magus of the City', *Guardian*, 23 January 1997. While many newspaper reviews repeat the same astonishment or bafflement at Sinclair's work, Wood offers an account of *Lights Out* that offers praise for Sinclair's style, while acknowledging that his 'anarchist-leftism' hides a deep conservatism that is revealed in his psychogeographical conceits that, firstly, do not take themselves seriously, and, secondly, try to turn politics to magic and vice versa.

OTHER TEXTS

Ackroyd, Peter, 'Cockney Visionaries', *Independent*, 18 December 1993.
—— *Hawksmoor* (London: Penguin, 1993).
Benjamin, Walter, *Charles Baudelaire: A Lyric Poet in the Era of High Capitalism* (London: New Left Books, 1973).
Blake, William, *The Poems of William Blake*, ed. W. H. Stevenson (London and NewYork: Longman/Norton, 1971).
Blazwick, Iwona, et al. (eds), *An Endless Adventure ... An Endless Passion ... An Endless Banquet: A Situationist Scrapbook* (London and New York: ICA/Verso, 1989).
Bloom, Clive, *Cult Fiction: Popular Reading and Pulp Theory* (Basingstoke and London: Macmillan, 1996).
Botting, Fred, *Gothic* (London and New York: Routledge, 1996).
Bourdieu, Pierre, 'The Field of Cultural Production, or The Economic World Reversed', in Bourdieu, *The Field of Cultural Production* (Cambridge: Polity Books, 1993), 29–73.
Butts, Mary, *The Crystal Cabinet: My Childhood at Salterns* (Manchester: Carcanet, 1988).
Catling, Brian, 'Spread Table, Spread Meal, Drink and Bread', an interview by Ian Hunt, *Parataxis*, 4 (Summer 1993), 42–57.
Cobbett, William, *Rural Rides*, vol. 1 (London: Dent, 1966)
Conrad, Joseph, *Heart of Darkness* (London: Penguin, 1983).
Cooper, David (ed.), *The Dialectics of Liberation* (Harmondsworth: Penguin, 1968)
Damon, S. Foster, *A Blake Dictionary* (Hanover and London: University Press of New England, 1998).
Dollimore, Jonathan, 'Art in Time of War: Towards a Contemporary Aesthetic', in John J. Joughin and Simon Malpas (eds), *The New Aestheticism* (Manchester and New York: Manchester University Press, 2003), 36–50.
Downes, Kerry, *Hawksmoor* (London: Thames and Hudson, 1970).
Hirsch, Hartmut, 'A Novel of a Future: Textual Strategies and Political Discourse in Recent Utopian Fiction in English', in Richard Todd and Luisa Flora (eds), *Theme Parks, Rainforests and Sprouting Wastelands* (Amsterdam and Atlanta: Editions Rodopi, BV, 2000).
Howell, Michael and Peter Ford, *The True History of the Elephant Man* (Harmondsworth: Penguin, 1980).
Lambrianou, Tony, *Inside the Firm* (London and Basingstoke: Pan Books, 1991).
Lehan, Richard, *The City in Literature: An Intellectual and Cultural History* (Berkeley, Los Angeles and London: University of California Press, 1998).

Lyotard, Jean-François, *The Lyotard Reader*, ed. Andrew Benjamin (Oxford: Blackwell, 1989).

McHale, Brian, *Postmodernist Fiction* (London and New York: Routledge, 1987).

Mengham, Rod, *An Introduction to Contemporary Fiction* (Cambridge: Polity Press, 1999).

Moi, Toril (ed.), *The Kristeva Reader* (Oxford: Blackwell, 1986).

Mottram, Eric, *William Burroughs: The Algebra of Need* (London: Marion Boyars, 1977).

Preliminary Problems in Constructing a Situation, from *Situationniste Internationale*, 1 (1958), on www. unpopular.demon.co.uk/lpa/ words.

Sullivan, J. P. (ed.), *Ezra Pound* (Harmondsworth: Penguin, 1970).

Tester, Keith (ed.), *The Flâneur* (London and New York: Routledge, 1994).

Watkins, A. *The Old Straight Track* (London: Abacus, 1974).

Wesling, D., 'The Poetry of Edward Dorn' in ed. Butterfield, RW, Modern American Poetry (Vision and Barnes and Noble, London and Totowa, 1984), pp. 218–233.

Wright, Patrick, 'Abysmal Heights' (1993), in Michael Miles, Tim Hall, and Iain Borden (eds), *The Big City Reader* (London and New York: Routledge, 2000), 174–9.

Index

Acker, Kathy, 10
Ackroyd, Peter, 1–5, 12, 19, 30, 42, 52
Archer, Jeffrey, 7, 87
Arendt, Hannah, 41
Ashmole, Elias, 87–8
Atkins, Marc, 10, 11, 86

Baker, Brian, 86, 89
Ballard, J. G., 14–15, 19, 41
Barnes, Julian, 5
Barry, Peter, 9–10, 16, 30, 85, 89
Bateson, Gregory, 8
Baudelaire, Charles, 84
Baudrillaud, Jean, 7
Beckett, Samuel, 71
Benjamin, Walter, 85
Bicknell, Renchi, 15, 19
Blair, Tony, 89
Blake, William, 2, 28, 32, 34, 38, 39–40, 67, 70, 90
Bloom, Clive, 44–5
Boadicea, 90
Bond, Robert, 87, 89, 92
Borges, J. L., 30, 42
Bourdieu, Pierre, 18, 84
Bowen, Stella, 61
Brakhage, Stan, 31
Brooker, Peter, 62
Bunyan, John, 25
Burroughs, William, 5, 9, 12, 42, 44, 45, 49, 69, 72, 79
Butts, Mary, 61, 67–8
Bygraves, Max, 22–3

Calvino, Italo, 42, 56
Campbell, Ken, 19
Cardinal Heenan, 26
Carmichael, Stokely, 8
Carter, Angela, 5, 42, 54, 57, 59, 60
Catling, Brian, 10, 11, 13, 18, 19, 31, 46, 69, 79
Cauty, Jimmy, 19
Certeau, Michel, de, 86
Chambers, Iain, 55
Chatterton, Thomas, 90, 91
Chatwin, Bruce, 8
Churchill, Winston, 16
Clare, John, 13
Cobbett, William, 14
Cohen, Abraham, 30
Coleridge, Samuel Taylor, 80
Conan Doyle, Arthur, 45, 49, 61, 78, 90
Conrad, Joseph, 23, 54, 63–4
Cornell, George, 35, 36, 41
Cronenberg, David, 14–15

Damon, S. Foster, 34
De Quincey, Thomas, 30
Deakin, John, 21
Deleuze, Gilles, 1
Derrida, Jacques, 66
Dick, Philip K., 47
Dickens, Charles, 54, 73
Dollimore, Jonathan, 92
Dorn, Edward, 35, 80
Drummond, Bill, 19
Dun, Aidan (Andrew), 89–92

Eco, Umberto, 77
Eliot, T. S., 60, 61

Fisher, Allen, 10, 28–9, 30, 80, 90, 92
Fisher, Roy, 28
Foucault, Michel, 61
Frobenius, 79
Fuller, Peter, 87

Gascoyne, David, 90
Gill, Eric, 74, 80
Ginsberg, Allen, 8–9, 18, 80
Goldmark, Mark, 11
Graham W. S., 78
Griffiths, Bill, 10, 16, 19
Guattari, Felix, 1
Gull, William, 47–52, 53, 57
Gwilym, Daffyd ap, 80

Harvey, David, 33–4
Harvey, William, 88
Harwood, Lee, 11, 28
Hawking, Stephen, 35, 70–1, 90
Hawksmoor, Nicholas, 4, 29–31, 33
Hayley, William, 34
Healy, John, 19
Heidegger, Martin, 33, 81
Hewison, Robert, 68
Hinton, James, 50–1
Hitchings, Henry, 20–1, 74
Hodgson, William Hope, 6
Home, Stewart, 85, 91
Hughes, Howard, 40
Hunt, Brothers, 34

Ignatius, Father, 74, 80

Jack the Hat (McVitie), 2, 35, 38, 87
Jack the Ripper, 2, 30, 44–54, 55, 56–8
Jackson, Kevin, 19, 92

James, P. D., 86
Jones, David, 11, 13, 74, 76–7, 79, 80
Joyce, James, 55

Kafka, Franz, 46
Kaveney, Roz, 42
Keats, John, 32
Keiller, Patrick, 88
Kelly, Marie Jeanette, 57
Kennedy, J. F., 47
Kenner, Hugh, 78–9
Kerouac, Jack, 47, 79
Kilvert, Francis, 80
King Cole, 64
King Harold, 38
Knight, Stephen, 47–8, 49, 50
Kray twins, 2, 30, 32, 35–41
Kristeva, Julia, 1
Kureishi, Hanif, 63

Laing, R. D., 8
Lambrianou, Tony, 6, 40, 41
Landor, Walter, Savage, 13, 73–4, 80
Lezard, Nicholas, 1, 42
Lichtenstein, Rachel, 9
Litvinoff, David, 8
Litvinoff, Emanuel, 7, 19
Lovecraft, H.P., 57

MacSweeney, Barry, 16, 90, 91, 92
Machen, Arthur, 43–4, 78, 80
Makin, Richard, 87
Malory, Sir Thomas, 81
Marks, Howard, 7, 23
McCartney, Paul, 11
McHale, Brian, 56
McKean, David, 11, 19
Merrick, Joseph (The Elephant Man), 52–3
Minton, John, 21
Moorcock, Michael, 5, 12, 42, 54, 81

Moore, Nicholas, 83, 84
Moseley, Billy, 38
Murdoch, Iris, 41

Nabokov, Vladimir, 71
Newton, Andrew, 75
Nuttall, Jeff, 8

O'Brien, Flann, 6
Oliver, Douglas, 10, 40–1
Olson, Charles, 8, 27–8, 80
Ondaatje, Michael, 35

Pascal, Blaise, 41
Pelham, Prudence, 76–7
Petit, Chris, 7, 12, 15, 19
Phillips, Tom, 48
Pinter, Harold, 9, 18
Pocahontas, 64
Poe, Edgar Allen, 54, 57
Potter, Rachel, 25, 59, 69–70
Pound, Ezra, 17, 18, 27, 39, 78–9, 80
Presley, Elvis, 39
Prince Eddy, 47
Prince Lee Boo, 64
Princess Anne, 26
Prynne, J. H., 6, 11, 13

Raban, Jonathan, 89
Rawlinson, Mark, 84
Raworth, Tom, 87
Raymond, Derek, 7, 19, 86, 88
Rendell, Ruth, 77
Reynolds, Simon, 20–1
Riley, Denise, 10
Riley, Peter, 83, 84, 87
Rimbaud, Arthur, 90
Rodinsky, David, 9–10, 13, 18, 65–7, 89
Rushdie, Salman, 4, 63

Sage, Lorna, 8
Scott, Norman, 75

Shelley, Mary, 90
Shelley, Percy Bysshe, 90
Sickert, Walter, 48
Sinclair, Iain
    Autistic Poses, 3
    Bridewell readings, the, 19
    Conductors of Chaos, 10, 11, 18, 80, 84
    Crash, 14–15
    Dark Lanthorns, 9–10, 14
    Dining on Stones, 9, 13, 22–4, 60
    Downriver, 5, 21, 23, 42, 43, 50, 54–72, 76, 83–4
    Ebbing of the Kraft, The, 10
    Edge of the Orison, 13
    Falconer, The, 12
    Flesh Eggs & Scalp Metal, 10
    Jack Elam's Other Eye, 10
    Kodak Mantra Diaries, 8–9, 11, 15, 91
    LAND/OR, 13, 80
    Landor's Tower, 11, 12–14, 16–17, 20, 43–4, 72–82
    Lights Out for the Territory, 7–8, 11, 16, 18, 37, 41, 83–93
    Liquid City, 10
    London: City of Disappearances, 13
    London Orbital, 15–16, 18, 19, 55, 83–9
        launch, 19
        TV 'road movie', 19
    Lud Heat, 2, 11, 15, 16, 17, 25–33, 40, 83, 90
    'Necromancer's A-Z, The', 4–5
    Penguin Modern Poets 10, 10
    Radon Daughters, 6–7, 11, 87
    'Red Eye', 90
    'Return of the Reforgotten, The', 11
    Rodinsky's Room, 9, 14, 17
    Saddling the Rabbit, 10
    'Shamanism of Intent, The', 19

Sixty Miles Out, 13
Slow Chocolate Autopsy, 11–12
Sorry Meniscus, 14
Study in Scarlet, A, (Conan
    Doyle, A.), 48–9
Suicide Bridge, 2, 3, 32–41
Verbals, The, 19, 92
'white chapel' novels, the, 12,
    72–3
White Chappell, Scarlet Tracings,
    3–5, 11, 41, 42, 44–54, 56–8,
    61, 75, 81
White Goods, 10, 13, 22
Stevenson, Robert Louis, 32, 52
Stoker, Bram, 88
Stone, Martin, 10
Swift, Graham, 4

Tenniel, John, 61
Tester, Keith, 85
Thatcher, Margaret, 5, 60, 64, 68,
    73, 88

Thompson, Hunter S., 8
Thorpe, Jeremy, 13, 73, 75
Torrance, Chris, 13, 28, 79
Tradescant, John, 87–8
Treves, Frederick, 52–3

Vaughan, Henry, 13, 75, 80
Vaughan, Thomas, 80
Verlaine, Paul, 90
Vine, Barbara, 77–8, 81, 82

Waite, Terry, 73, 81
Watkins, Alfred, 16–17, 29, 73, 78
Watkins, Vernon, 13, 80
Watson, Ben, 87, 89, 92
Wells, H. G., 88
Williams, John, 38–9
Williams, William Carlos, 27
Williamson, Aaron, 11, 18
Wood, James, 8, 19–20, 21

Yeats, W. B., 79, 92

DH

828.
914
09
SHE

Printed in the United Kingdom by
Lightning Source UK Ltd., Milton Keynes
142165UK00001B/33/A